# NOVELS OF
# BOTSWANA
## IN ENGLISH, 1930-2006

# NOVELS OF
# BOTSWANA
## IN ENGLISH, 1930-2006

## MARY S. LEDERER

AFRICAN HERITAGE PRESS

NEW YORK   LAGOS   LONDON

2014

**AFRICAN HERITAGE PRESS**

First Edition, African Heritage Press, 2014

Library of Congress catalog number: 2014934099

Lederer, Mary S.

Cover Design: Dapo Ojoade

ISBN: 978-1-940729-15-2

For Bruce

# CONTENTS

Acknowledgements
ix

Introduction
1

There Was No Place Like Home—Botswana Novels in English
21

"Literary" Novels of Botswana
51

Paper Safari—Adventure Novels of Botswana
91

Lady Detectives—Alexander McCall Smith and Lauri Kubuitsile
115

The Possibility of Justice—Bessie Head and Unity Dow
135

Conclusion
161

Appendix: New Publications Since 2007
167

Works Cited
169

Index
177

# ACKNOWLEDGEMENTS

I would like to thank the following for their assistance: Michelle Commeyras, Grant Lilford, Reshoketjoe Lilford, and Felix Mnthali and Leloba Molema of the University of Botswana English Department for reading versions of the manuscript and making very helpful suggestions; the University of Botswana, where I was lecturer in English until 2005, for sponsoring me to attend a number of conferences where several of these chapters were presented in a preliminary form; my cousin Mark Lederer and my uncle Richard Lederer (not the author of *Anguished English*) of Madison, Wisconsin, my friend Wendy Belcher of Princeton, New Jersey, and my father-in-law, R. G. T. Bennett, of Christchurch, New Zealand, for library assistance in getting materials that were not available to me in Botswana; Neil Parsons, formerly of the University of Botswana History Department, for introducing me to *A Desert of Salt* and other books and thus helping the idea for this book take shape; the editorial team at African Heritage Press for carefully reading and editing the manuscript; the Wednesday Ladies, especially Leloba Molema, Nobantu Rasebotsa, Johanna Stiebert, Laurel Lanner, Maitseo Bolaane, Pinkie Mekgwe, Reshoketjoe Lilford, and Treasa Galvin; my family, of course; and most of all, my husband, Bruce Bennett, who read most of the novels under discussion, commented on various drafts of every chapter, discussed the project with me continually, and encouraged and supported me in every possible way. *Ke itumetse.*

# INTRODUCTION

"A nation without a past is a lost nation, and a people without a past is a people without a soul."
—Sir Seretse Khama, first President of the Republic of Botswana[1]

Twenty-five years ago, many people probably thought Botswana was one of South Africa's homelands, confusing—or combining—it with its "neighbor" Bophuthatswana. Part of the confusion of where—and what—Botswana is stems from its past and its unusual status in the colonial empire. Part of the confusion probably also arises from the rather quiet nature of the place itself, though there are, of course, lots of famous things in Botswana. United States presidents make high-profile

---

1. Graduation speech as Chancellor of University of Botswana, Lesotho, and Swaziland on 15 May 1970 (*Botswana Daily News*, 19 May 1970, supplement, qtd. in Tlou, Parsons, and Henderson 314).

1

visits here; Britain's Prince Harry visits the Okavango Delta frequently, and Alexander McCall Smith, with his No. 1 Ladies' Detective Agency novels, has recently made Botswana possibly best known as the home of Mma Precious Ramotswe. Consequently, many tour companies now offer short city tours of Mma Ramotswe's Gaborone, and Anthony Minghella's film and television series have helped raise Gaborone's profile. National Geographic videos detail the lives of Botswana's lions and elephants, which no doubt fuel the tourist interest in and expectations of "wild" Botswana. However, Botswana is also the home to a former Miss Universe; it is one of the largest diamond producers in the world, where many people drive brand-spanking-new Mercedes Benz 4X4s out to their remote cattle posts, and where a school may be closed because of attacks by a *tokoloshe*.[2]

It is a society in transition. Botswana has a stable political past, and its present sparkles with the newness of diamonds and the wealth that they bring, but great wealth lives side by side with great poverty. It has a strong patriarchy, but that patriarchy faces strong challenges from women who occupy positions of power (in 2007, Botswana ranked sixth in the world with the percentage of women who control businesses as CEOs, etc.; see *Grant Thornton International Business Report 2007: Global Overview*), but where those same women are still expected to retain control of domestic responsibilities and be mothers above all else.

Botswana is a place that looks empty, and the mythology of emptiness is important to the tourist industry (where else in Africa can you get so close to those lions and elephants?) but, as anyone who has traveled in Botswana will know, people here live everywhere. More than occasionally, they have been

---

2. A *tokoloshe* (also spelled *thokolosi*) is a small supernatural being that does the bidding of a witch, usually requested or paid for by someone with a grudge.

relocated,[3] and the appearance of emptiness is sometimes a result of such removals. In 2006, the High Court upheld the rights of a group of KhoeSan to remain in the Central Kalahari Game Reserve (CKGR), after the government tried to relocate them out of the Reserve. The government's argument rested on two points: first, that it was not cost effective to provide amenities (water, schools, and clinics) in the park and thus "develop" the scattered groups of people. Development is an important concept in national policy, and discussions of which policies will or will not develop the people of the country occupy much public debate. Development is almost always assumed to be good (i.e., there is little discussion about the nature of development itself). Even Batswana who reject Western values and espouse "tradition" believe in the intrinsic value of development, and San are thus frequently derided for their desire to preserve their "primitive" way of life.

The government's second argument in its defense was that the presence of people living in the park is disruptive to tourist activity—an early argument when the CKGR was first established made the point that the people living there were part of the natural environment. Now that is an unacceptable prospect, although ironically San are often portrayed in tourist literature as a feature of the Botswana African experience. In a strange conflict of interest, development is understood to hinder development: tourism will succeed if people think they can see some version of "old" or "original" Africa. At the same time that public opinion expresses incomprehension about a lack of will to develop, its official institutions promote a primitive quality as part of Botswana's attraction: where else will you find people hunting large game with Stone-Age bows and

---

3. See, for example, Keamogetswe and Lesie Kwere's account of their relocations in "We Will Be Leasing for Ourselves."

arrows, even if most hunters now use guns? This clash, and the fact that it seems to pass unremarked in the press, is characteristic of many aspects of Botswana; the cultural confusion that results when cultural traits are absorbed without any awareness of the diversity of their origins mirrors a similar confusion in the West. A number of years ago, an IMAX movie about "the African savanna" was circulating in theaters in the United States. The movie began as do most nature movies about Africa: showing a continent of marvelous wildlife. As the movie unfolded, however, the telescoping effect that was created as the camera moved from the panoramic (the Great Rift Valley as seen from the air) to ever smaller "units" was astonishing: herds of wildebeest, then of elephant, then the sound of cow bells in the darkness, then suddenly Maasai dancing around a fire. Africa as a place looms very large in the non-African imagination (as well as in the African one), and this image is fostered by tourist boards in countries that wish to make money from safaris. The IMAX movie produced a visual image of people and cows and wildebeest as undifferentiated "fauna of Africa" that is often unquestioned in contemporary public and even academic debate about the nature—characteristic or personality, if you will—of Africa. Nevertheless, such unquestioned images frequently, even today, find their way into tourist literature, including literature about Botswana. Tourist literature designed by Botswana government agencies ironically often presents the KhoeSan this same way, despite literary and other objections to such representations,[4] and despite the Botswana government's own arguments in the CKGR relocation lawsuit.

In his 1990 study *Theories of Africans: Francophone Literature and Anthropology in Africa*, Christopher Miller offers an argument

---

4. See Alexander McCall Smith's descriptions of the lion child in *Morality for Beautiful Girls* (105–10 and 222–24) and Bessie Head about science and San in *Maru* (11–12).

that anthropology (as well as history and sociological perspectives) are necessary if a Western reader is to read African literature fairly (4). He argues that literary theory itself, because it is the most privileged form of Western discourse (elevated above the material and representing the "realm of pure thought" [7]), could also describe the role of the Western reader: "detached, objective, universal, synthesizing, and...powerful" (7). While Miller acknowledges the paradox that reading literature through anthropology poses—anthropology is after all a Western discipline—he suggests that a successful reader of African literature must surrender to that paradox (21).

Such a surrender is not necessarily impossible, undesirable, or even uncommon. Students of French, German, English, and other literature are taught from an early stage to consider the context of the literature they are studying, although the problem of using one discipline (such as history) to understand another is not as problematic for Western students of other Western cultures. African literature, however, is often simply presented within the context of postcolonial studies (itself arguably a Western discourse), as if the continent had no history, no social structures, no diversity, no interest, and no lives of its own.

Miller describes this homogenization or the lack of differentiation as a problem in terms of what he describes as the choice that the colonized self faces: equality versus identity, or in simplified terms, ethic versus ethnic. A Marxian call for universalization, for example, is not a viable choice for most Africans, since equality requires them often to sacrifice their clan or ethnic identity, itself an important component of more general identity—and ethnic identity is often more important than even national identity (38). To illustrate this dilemma, Miller uses the example of the Guinean artist Fodéba Keïta's poetry. Miller points that in Fodéba's poetry, the ethical is in fact indebted to the ethnic (59), and that politics, as "the medium in which ethnicity and ethics interact" (65), is therefore necessary. This comes close to implying that relativism is an inevitable part of any society in general, and in particular an inevitable part of the study of any foreign literature. It becomes problematic as a hegemonic relationship in the case of Westerners looking at non-Western literature, and that is the paradox. In this argument, *Theories of Africans* itself must also therefore be a paradox, or at the very least a contradiction, but it is a contradiction and paradox that Miller himself practically (i.e., in practical terms) embraces.

Miller devotes an entire chapter of his book ("Ethnicity and Ethics") to exploring the problems and conditions of relativism, and makes what he calls "the bind of relativism" part of his undertaking:

> my response to the bind of relativism is neither to seek some miraculous solution to it nor to ignore the real problems it poses; relativism both underpins and undercuts an intellectual endeavor like this one. The mélange of questions, approaches, and sources that will fuel the readings that follow is a reflection of who I am (an American who has spent time living, teaching, researching, and travelling in Africa and who has been trained in the United States in the analysis of literary texts) and of what I have been able to see, read, and understand. It will display a continuing, if skeptical, interest in Western theoretical issues, especially when they claim competence in regard to Africa; this is to some extent a reflection of my milieu, but equally a reflection of the discursive field that exists in African studies. I will therefore not pretend to transcend or abandon the American academic scene, but from within it I will attempt a dialogue with another scene, whose issues and language are partially, *problematically*, different: francophone Africa. The result will be anything but a "pure product." (67)

This book is also not a pure product. I, too, am an American trained in the American university system, but I have lived and worked for nearly fifteen years in Botswana, after having worked only very briefly in the United States. I am still a *lekgoa*, not a *motho fêla* (*motho* = person, *fêla* = just or only; see discussion under Language Structure that follows), but I am more familiar with the intellectual environment of Botswana, and therefore my milieu is very different. My status as an "expert" on Botswana must certainly be suspect: I have been here long enough to recognize that I hardly know anything, but I have also been here long enough to recognize that many Western readings of southern African literature exhibit less understanding of the historical, social, and cultural context than they probably need. I am interested in the questions that Miller opens up about how ethnicity informs ethical outlook; I am interested in how and why national identity is promoted, and what challenges ethnicity makes to that national identity; I am interested in how the character of "Motswana" is defined and is changing in the twenty-first century.

## LANGUAGE STRUCTURE

Most southern African languages belong to the group of Bantu languages, in which nouns are divided into classes rather than genders. Nouns are classified or defined inter alia according to the degree of "human-ness" that the speaker wishes to emphasize. People who belong to the insider groups (such as Tswana) are identified by class-one nouns. Thus, the root "Tswana" identifies a specific set of characteristics. A person who identifies as Tswana[5] is thus a Motswana; plural, Batswana. The language is Setswana. In English, the word Tswana is

---

5. Common English usage of the root refers to someone who is ethnic Tswana, rather than a citizen, Motswana. In addition, Western academics commonly use the root forms of Bantu words (e.g., Zulu, Xhosa, Chewa, etc.).

commonly used as an adjective, but in Setswana itself, the root word *tswana* by itself does not make any sense because it is an incomplete word. A man is *monna* (plural, *banna*), and a woman is *mosadi* (plural, *basadi*). Most words used to denote people begin with *mo-* or, for plural, *ba-*.[6]

A major exception to this rule is for people who are outsiders, who frequently are described in a noun class of words that begin with *le-*. A white person is *lekgoa* (plural, *makgoa*); a Boer is *leburu* (plural, *maburu*), a German is *lejeremane* (plural, *majeremane*), and so on. Until the 1970s, this category also applied to the KhoeSan, who were referred to in the plural as *masarwa*. The change from *lesarwa* to *Mosarwa* (and *masarwa* to *Basarwa*) indicates an attempt to remove some of the stigma that attaches to people referred to by words beginning with *le-*, since one form of insult in Setswana is to refer to someone using a le- noun-class construction.

Of course, people from KhoeSan language groups should be called by their names: Naro, Bugakhoe, Ju/'hoan, and so forth. KhoeSan is a collective noun (like Bantu) that refers to people of two different backgrounds: Khoe and San. Many of these people dislike being referred to as San (or Khoe) since the wrong word insults them. Some insist on being referred to as San. The official Botswana term is Basarwa, referring to various groups of people who speak languages of the Khoe-San family; many people are satisfied with this appellation, and many are not. Some prefer to be called by the term Bushmen— even though that description is now both disliked by Western academics and regarded as impolite in the region—because of the fact that it is a very recognizable term to outsiders and

---

6. For a more comprehensive discussion of the structure of Setswana noun classes, see D. T. Cole, *An Introduction to Tswana Grammar* (Cape Town and Johannesburg, Longman Penguin Southern Africa, 1992 [1955]).

attracts Western attention. The following discussions will refer to "San," the term used in academic discourse, unless the individual group's name is known—and, in fact, most writers simply do not make the distinction.

## BACKGROUND TO BOTSWANA

The statement by Sir Seretse Khama that opens this introduction occupies an important place in the way Botswana sees itself and in the way the people of Botswana look back to their past; it is an important part of Botswana's developing mythology about itself. University of Botswana students of history frequently quote it (and misquote it) in order to justify their choice of research topic, and the "project" of defining a Botswana national character based on Botswana's past influences nearly every aspect of life here.

But "what" is Botswana?[7] The name itself means the place of the Tswana peoples (*bo-*), but that name also strikes at the core of the problem of defining Botswana's national character: it is a place of many people, not just Tswana. The country itself is mostly desert (the Kalahari Desert) and people live everywhere, but most of the water and resources are found along the eastern border. In the north, the Chobe/Zambezi river divides Botswana from Zambia, but many of the people who live there have familial links across the river. The Kalanga of northeast Botswana are closely related to the Ndebele of Zimbabwe (who are themselves related to many people in northern South Africa). Nomadic groups of people still travel through the desert, and the Okavango Delta is home to Herero and Hambukushu people (and other smaller groups) who fled from persecution and civil war further west and north in Namibia and Angola. In

---

7. See Thomas Tlou and Alec Campbell, *History of Botswana* (Gaborone: Macmillan Botswana, 1997 [1984]) for a thorough history of the country.

the south, other groups of people who speak dialects of Setswana (the BaRolong, BaNgwaketse, BaKwena, and others) have been settled for a long time.

Thus, when missionaries and hunters arrived in this part of southern Africa, they found a great mix of people coexisting—or not—in what probably seemed to them an extremely harsh environment. Hunters, of course, found the place teeming with wildlife, and safari accounts from the nineteenth century tell of incredible slaughter, always with the assistance of a "native" guide. When the missionaries arrived, they found groups of people living in not very permanent camps (depending on the water supply), who were more or less willing to hear them out regarding the new religion.

But the land held no obvious riches. When Cecil Rhodes began to move north in his quest to expand the empire from Cape to Cairo, he saw in Botswana only a large, flat, dusty place that would have to be traveled through, preferably by railroad, in order to get to better, more important places further north. When Rhodes and the Boers from South Africa tried to incorporate Botswana into their plans, the Bechuanaland Protectorate was established in order to preserve the way north for expansion of the British Empire. The identity of the place was thus shaped from the beginning of the colonial period by a perception that it contained nothing of value to the empire or the West, that this part of the interior of southern Africa was simply a vast emptiness that had to be got through somehow.

It now appears that the British, who nominally governed the protectorate from 1885 to 1966, at first assumed that the Protectorate would at some point have to be turned over to the Cape Colony, or the Union of South Africa (which absorbed the Cape Colony when the Union was established in 1910), or possibly even Rhodesia. That this handover did not happen is due to a number of factors, including the resistance of the BaNgwato regent Tshekedi Khama, one of the most powerful chiefs in the country, as well as growing British opposition to South African policies. Things came to a crisis in the 1950s when Seretse Khama, heir to the BaNgwato chieftainship, suddenly married Ruth Williams, a white British woman. The South African government tried to put pressure on the British government to prevent the marriage or possibly to force Seretse to divorce Ruth, and Tshekedi Khama himself, who was Seretse's uncle, opposed the marriage on the grounds that Williams was an outsider. Eventually, Seretse Khama, despite his great popular support, was forced to abdicate his chieftainship. That popular support nevertheless made it possible for him to remain in politics, and he was the first president of Botswana upon independence in 1966.

The interference of South Africa (and, it later transpired, British willingness to allow it) had another important effect on the initial shape of "Botswana." In the face of utter hostility to the south, a war of liberation in the east (Rhodesia/Zimbabwe), and South African occupation of South-West Africa (Namibia), Botswana felt that it needed to present a unified, nonethnic front. English was made the official language (as in other former British colonies in the region), but Setswana was made the "national language" (a policy now being contested by a number of people who speak different languages). Seretse Khama had to walk a very fine line between resistance to South African interference and dependence on South African imports. The national character of Botswana thus was held to subsume within it the diversity of the people who actually lived in there: a person was a Motswana first and a Ngwato, Kalanga, KhoeSan, even white, second.

After 1994, however, everything changed. South Africa now described itself as the Rainbow Nation, and as a gesture toward the importance of all groups that lived there, eleven official languages were identified (the practice of using these languages differs somewhat from the model in a country with only two such languages). Botswana's enemy no longer existed in its old form, and without the need to present that unified front, tears have begun to appear in the social fabric. Public debate rages about whether students should learn in Setswana at the primary-school level, or should they learn in their mother tongues—SiYei, iKalanga, SeSubiya, and so on. At the same time, a 2005 study (Afrobarometer[8]) showed that a large majority of people identify Setswana as the language they most often speak at home. Ethnic or tribal identity is confused in other ways, too. After centuries of intermarriage, the differences between "Tswana," "Kalanga," "Kgalagadi," and everyone else are beginning to blur.

The meaning of "Motswana" is further complicated by the fact that a number of groups such as the Ngwato, Kgatla, Ngwaketse, and others are also ethnic Tswana. A person of Ngwato background would then also be Tswana as well as a Motswana citizen of Botswana, but a person of Kalanga background would only be a Motswana citizen of Botswana, not Tswana. In addition, although KhoeSan still suffer great oppression and indignity, the legacy of their former status, including often as concubines and even slaves, can be seen in the shape and complexion of many faces around the country.

This fleeting summary of Botswana's history gives a glimpse into the multilayered and multifaceted roots of the nature and perhaps problem of identity in Botswana. The problem of Botswana's identity can, of course, also be situated within discussions of nationalism. In the 1960s, when many African nations became independent, defining national identity played a role

---

8. For a summary of the findings of this study, see the University of Botswana History website at http://www.thuto.org/ubh/bw/society/afrob1.htm. The complete report for Botswana can also be downloaded from http://www.afrobarometer.org/data/data-by-country/botswana/item/368-botswana-round-3-data-2005.

in almost every aspect of national life, including in literature. Because independence fixed colonial borders, national identity was often celebrated at the expense of other sorts of identity, as was also the case with Botswana. But often, ethnic identity remained strong, even in the face of borders that cut through ethnic or tribal regions. Botswana is no different. The first and most obvious absurdity of this situation arose when the capital of the Bechuanaland Protectorate was established in Mafeking (now Mafikeng) just south of the Protectorate's border.[9] The southern border of Botswana cuts directly through the lands of the BaRolong, and even today many people do not bother with border formalities when they wish to visit their close relatives over the border, with whom they often share fields and other property. In the north and northeast, the Kalanga and BaBirwa face a similar dilemma with respect to family living in Zimbabwe. The complications increase during times of political or economic crisis, when people flee to their family across the border in Botswana, but do not have legal permission to reside here.

Thus, Botswana nationalism today faces a very difficult challenge in people's growing ethnic identification as well as in regional and continental calls for a pan-African structure. In 1968, David Rubadiri wrote in an article on national literature that identity was not national but spiritual (52–53): a person's beliefs and habits do not adjust themselves according to artificial (and often also arbitrary) borders. Rubadiri's statement

---

9. The capital of Botswana—Gaborone—did not exist as a city before independence in 1966. Until independence, it was known as Gaberones, where Chief Gaborone stayed, and the administrative structures that are now on the outskirts of the city were considered to be in Gaborone's village (now a section of the city known simply as "Village"). Gaborone was chosen as the site for Botswana's capital city because it was near a reliable source of water and also because it had no affiliation with a major group.

resonates today, more than forty years later, in the way people in Botswana see themselves and their relationships to other Batswana.

## BOTSWANA LITERATURE AND NATIONAL LITERATURE

An important thread that runs through many of the novels considered in this book is the idea and ideal of the morality of Botswana society: what morals define the Botswana character—at least as local writers see it. This characteristic is most evident in the novels of Andrew Sesinyi and Galesiti Baruti, who express obvious dismay at the state of current Botswana society and long for a return to the old ways and the old morals. That those morals themselves are subject to debate and reformulation is not really an issue for them. Even Alexander Mc-Call Smith identifies the question of morality in his series, but Precious Ramotswe is not an advocate of a wholesale return to the old ways, since under those ways she would have suffered in a bad marriage and would have been unable to open her detective agency. Modern women writing in Botswana cast a more critical eye on the morals that Sesinyi and Baruti champion, but they, too, criticize contemporary Botswana society in the context of those morals.

In his consideration of British national literature, Antony Easthope considers the problem of autobiography vis-à-vis narratives of national identity, which can use the past to "imagine a future which confers on us an identity in the present" (151). Easthope's statement recalls Seretse Khama's statement about the nation's soul, but it also provides a way to begin a survey of Botswana literature. Botswana writers imagine a past that simultaneously imagines an identity for the future. Writers like Sesinyi and Baruti look at the structures and ideals of the past and try in their writing to integrate them with the Botswana identity of the present as way of ensuring not only that the present is "modern" but that the future still resembles the past. Other writers, most notably Bessie Head and Unity Dow, cast a critical eye on the past that consequently brings under scrutiny present social structures and mores, and the future that they seem to hope for is one in which the morals of the past are re-modeled more substantially to suit the needs of a changed (and changing) society.

Sesinyi and Baruti would appear to have a more nationalist project. Their Botswana is clearly structured with the capital Gaborone at the center, surrounded by the rural areas that feed it. The identity of the modern nation of Botswana is thus tied closely to the modern, postindependence capital, a city that did not even exist before 1965. This identification presents a para-dox, of course: the novels that most celebrate the past put the new city at their center. This idea of a national entity is again undercut by both Head and Dow, who repeatedly make refer-ence in their work to the problem of borders cutting through clan/tribe/family configurations. For them, identity cannot and does not rest in a place where Gaborone is the capital, because that city is an artificial one and because people live with their families in places like Mochudi and Serowe, more "traditional" settlements that have been in existence much longer.

Of course, Setswana literature also defines national identity in other, undoubtedly more significant, ways. Richard Björn-son, in his study of Cameroonian national literature, discusses the importance of print (newspapers, books, etc.) in fostering a national identity[10]: "Literate culture has played a crucial role in fostering a heightened sense of national consciousness be-cause it has helped establish the shared references by means of which people recognize their participation in a specific universe of discourse" (xi). In Botswana the print culture is largely in

---

10. See also Björnson, chapter 1.

English; what is not in English is almost exclusively in Setswana. Print culture thus reinforces the hegemony of Setswana, as well as English, over other local languages, and so it is not surprising that so many people identify Setswana as the language they speak at home, regardless of what they state as their ethnic identity.

This survey does not consider Setswana literature, which is not at all a marginal or small body of literature. However, Setswana literature in Botswana as a corpus and in its very language raises questions of national and linguistic identity in ways that are beyond the scope of this book.[11] Generally in Botswana, writers who use English are (as are writers elsewhere in Africa) often aiming for a larger audience.[12] Their examination of Botswana's self-identity will be compared with what other writers from outside the country see.

## CHOICE AND ARRANGEMENT OF TEXTS

This book is intended as a survey and an introduction. It is, to the best of my knowledge, the first book-length study to be written on the literature about Botswana. It is particularly about how Botswana is represented in novels by writers of different nationalities. When this project began, the body of novels in English by Batswana writers was too small to consider by itself (although it is growing), and while English novels by Batswana deal (for the most part) with Botswana, the place features in a surprising amount and type of literature from outside the region. One question to consider is to what extent literature by non-Batswana reinforces Botswana's own image of itself.

---

11. In addition, the corpus of Setswana literature extends well beyond the borders of Botswana, since the majority of Setswana speakers are South African.

12. This point, of course, raises the issue of who controls publishing and who can afford to buy books.

The criteria for this book comprise novels for adults in which the setting is substantial and recognizable.

This discussion is limited to prose fiction for two reasons. First, drama in southern Africa is still very much a performance art, and dramatic texts are not read so much as they are considered for performance. Second, poetry and short stories are huge and growing genres. Much poetry (as is also the case with drama) is written in Setswana. Sol Plaatje has also been included, although he is not technically a Botswana writer; he was South African (and is indeed usually claimed by South Africans as one of them), but his novel *Mhudi* was important in forming early understanding of the Tswana identity,[13] and in addition he was a very important scholar of the Setswana language. He has been included because at the time he wrote, the understandings of "South Africa," "Bechuanaland," and so forth, were not as clearly defined by the borders they are today (e.g., the administrative capital of the Bechuanaland Protectorate was in Mafeking, outside the Protectorate).

Botswana's most famous writer is of course Bessie Head. Her books are frequently included in university-level courses on postcolonial, women's, African, and world literature. However, because the present book is an introductory survey, Head's novels have been included in chapters where they seemed thematically appropriate rather than being grouped in a separate chapter (*A Bewitched Crossroad* in the next chapter on Tswana identity; and *When Rain Clouds Gather* in chapter 6, with the novels of Unity Dow, on women in Tswana society). References to her other works (*Maru, A Question of Power*, and *The Cardinals*) are included, but those novels are not as deeply concerned with the themes of the other chapters in this book. In addition, to devote

---

13. See Grant Lilford, "*Motswana ke mang?* Tswana Culture and Values in Plaatje, Head, and McCall Smith."

a whole chapter to her novels would be to open up a large new set of issues and points of discussion that are beyond the scope of this book. Whole books have been written about her work, and the bibliography of articles about her writing is too extensive to even include here. For readers who want to know more about Botswana's most famous writer (and indeed one of the most important African writers ever), Gillian Stead Eilersen's thorough biography *Bessie Head: Thunder Behind Her Ears. Her Life and Writing* will provide insight into Head's life and work, and give new readers a place to start.

Bessie Head's importance for Botswana literature in particular is unclear. Certainly, many people in Serowe knew she was a writer, and even today Serowe is familiar with her name and her legacy. The Khama III Memorial Museum in Serowe holds all her letters and has a "Bessie Head Room," where visitors can see a re-creation of the room in which she wrote. When I arrived in Botswana in 1997, many of my students at the University of Botswana had never heard of her; this has since changed because the English Department now includes her works in a number of its classes and offers an entire fourth-year seminar devoted to her writing. Many people find her work somewhat inaccessible, especially and not surprisingly *A Question of Power*, which is the title they are most likely to have heard of. An abridged version of *When Rain Clouds Gather* is taught at secondary school, and that version has been translated into Setswana, but the latter is difficult to get. Head's history of Serowe, *Serowe: Village of the Rain Wind*, has been promoted as a suitable text for senior secondary pupils; however, even though it is in print, it is hard to obtain, except in second-hand bookshops. The sad irony is that Bessie Head is probably better known in the rest of the world than she is here in the country where she chose to make her home.

This book is not the first word on Botswana literature, and I certainly do not mean it to be the last. There will be many errors and omissions, all of them my own, but I hope that my colleagues in Botswana will take up this challenge to set me straight, to consider Botswana's literature in a regional and continental context, and to put Botswana, including but not exclusively Bessie Head, more firmly and visibly on the world literary map.

## THERE WAS NO PLACE LIKE HOME—
## BOTSWANA NOVELS IN ENGLISH

Batswana have a very strong sense of themselves as being from Botswana. The place as "home" occupies a very central part of Tswana identity, and most Batswana who work or study abroad look forward (more strongly than most people) to returning. Nothing is as good as it is at home in Botswana.

Botswana novels in English reflect this nostalgic, and somewhat uncritical, view of place. Many people feel, like Dorothy in *The Wizard of Oz*, that there's no place like home. At the time of this writing, the body of novels by Batswana in English is relatively small. More people write in English about Botswana than from it. This situation is changing, of course, as Botswana's population becomes more literate in English, and as earlier, mission-educated models who preferred to write in Setswana are replaced by a more "Pan-African" model of writing in (and being translated into) English. Particularly striking is the number of women who are beginning to write, and to write critically about their own society.

Part of this strong sense of identity as tied to geographical location undoubtedly comes from the legacy of Khama the Great, who in the late nineteenth and early twentieth centuries fashioned much of the future nation out of disparate groups of people in the face of threats from both the Afrikaners and the British. Khama was a strong proponent of Christianity; he was baptized, and he abolished a number of customs and habits that he considered inappropriate in the context of the new beliefs, such as initiation rites and brewing traditional beer. Popular perception of him as a good and moral man is part of his legacy, and "moral" describes an important part of the place Botswana.

How, then, do the novels that are written in English by Batswana reflect Botswana morality and Botswana as a place? Certainly, Khama's strong legacy constitutes an important aspect of Botswana literature in English. There are possibly other, historical, reasons for this tendency to "moralize," having to do with Botswana's "exceptional" status in the region and in understanding its history.

Neil Parsons, in a response to Ken Good's discussion of Botswana's exceptionality,[1] believes that Botswana "can only be understood as a southern African society in the context of neighbouring countries; and while it has been exceptional in the last quarter century, that exceptionality is today [1993] being lost" (74). Botswana most certainly is a southern African society, both in terms of its cultural relationships to South Africans (for example, more Setswana speakers live in South Africa than in Botswana itself), as well as in terms of the overwhelming influence that South Africa exercises over the whole region.

It was only in 1891 that a strategic overlordship of the area was converted, even in principle, to an internal administration,

---

1. See Kenneth Good, "Interpreting the Exceptionality of Botswana."

and in 1895 the northern half of the Protectorate was added. Even after 1895 the Protectorate was allowed a measure of internal autonomy, most importantly perhaps in the form of the *kgotla* and the chiefly power that was part of *kgotla*. *Kgotla* refers to both a place and a system of consultation with elder men of the tribe. There is some debate about just how participatory it was (e.g., debates concerning how the *kgotla* has changed to reflect historical and social change), but certainly women were excluded, as were men from subordinate groups, although they no longer are. After independence, Seretse Khama gradually eroded the power of the chiefs, and Batswana today are grappling with the consequences of that erosion, which stripped power from a rural elite. Nevertheless, the *kgotla* is still seen as an important part of village life, and is often cited as an example of what is valuable about the past by people who want to bring back the old custom. At almost every level of society, legitimate decisions must be at least represented as arrived at by consensus rather than by command.

Parsons identifies a number of aspects of Botswana history and explains both how they contribute to the exceptional nature of Botswana society and how they currently contribute to the changes taking place in the society. In other words, Botswana's exceptionality may have protected it from the more destructive effects of colonialism, but it also contributes to the difficulties Botswana faces today. For example, "Botswana is catching up with the colonial experience of its neighbours, with what it missed in the colonial period—massive land alienation" (80), an alienation that is not a result of racial discrimination but rather of the emergence of a new elite who accumulate land as well as cattle. This accumulation of traditional forms of wealth has contributed to the growing gap between the wealthy elite and the dispossessed majority. People move to the cities to find jobs in a familiar pattern of rural-urban migration (as does Pule in Sesinyi's *Love on the Rocks*) but their attachment to the communal land remains strong,[2] even if that attachment is no longer realistic or reflective of "reality." Some Botswana fiction, almost exclusively fiction by male writers, laments the erosion of tradition (in *Carjack*, for example, Sesinyi describes "the drone of the morning traffic of gleaming latest-model sedans, driven nonchalantly by a city population spoiled by a booming diamond-sales economy" [1]). These fictional worlds often prescribe an unrealistic, uncritical embrace of the good old days and a rejection of modern life that ignores the problematic nature of those same old days as well as the historical processes that have both kept Botswana peaceful and at the same time led to the current social instability. In addition, by embracing the past, people tend to forget that in that same past, Botswana hoped for a more developed future, one that is now here. This phenomenon is of course not particular to Botswana, but the representation of that morality in literature is a characteristic of Botswana literature in English. This chapter will look at some of the novels of Botswana to understand how Batswana see themselves and their relationship to their society. [3]

An important point to keep in mind in the consideration of "national" novels by Batswana writers is the pedagogical

---

2. When the first Botswana contestant and winner in the 1999 Miss Universe pageant, Mpule Kwelagobe, was asked during the early part of the competition what people in Botswana liked to do "for fun," she answered (undoubtedly to cheers all over Botswana), "You go to your cattle post. It is known that every Motswana has a cattle post full of cattle. So that's where you go!" (48th Miss Universe Pageant, Trinidad and Tobago, 26 May 1999). Kwelagobe's statement reflects the importance of cattle and the land in popular consciousness, and it reflects a very popular belief about what is normal—but in fact not actually common. Kwelagobe's assertion that "every Motswana" owns cattle obscures the reality about who owns cattle—and land—and who does not.
3. At a primary-school art exhibit that I attended in 2004, a number of pupils had drawn pictures of the "Gaborone of the future," many of

one. Richard Björnson identifies within Cameroonian literature a "sense of responsibility" that is "a crucial ingredient of the nation-building process," using the example of pamphlets that "employ fictionalized accounts of individual experience to promote morally responsible behavior in this context" (314). A Botswana example of such a pamphlet is Caleb Nondo's *Lethal Virus*, in which he presents a fictionalized picture of the way AIDS ravages the society, with the text promoting responsible attitudes towards HIV and the way it is spread. Nondo, a family physician in Gaborone, writes in his epilogue of his desire to halt the spread of this disease: "Perhaps, it is better to learn to be afraid. Then, maybe, the spread of AIDS will be defeated" (99). In case the moral is not clear, Nondo includes a final section at the end called "Points for discussion," which begins with the statement that "*Lethal Virus* is a cautionary tale which deals with the reality of HIV and AIDS," and ends with the assertion that "these are critical questions because, at the end of the day, our awareness of the reality of HIV and AIDS is our only guard against the disease. Awareness must lead to a change in life-style for us all" (100). Many novels are equally cautionary, if not quite so explicit.

This pedagogical—didactic, even—characteristic is not only a feature of Botswana literature. Joanna Sullivan notes the importance of didactic novels in Hausa (and other Nigerian) literature. She begins her argument by quoting Simon Gikandi and Emmanuel Obiechina, who both emphasize the important feature of African literature that the individual's life is not primarily psychologically but rather socially determined (qtd. in Sullivan 182–83). Characters in these novels are thus

---

which displayed the continuing popular enthusiasm for "development" as a kind of technotopia, including one picture that showed Gaborone with a skyline like New York City's, in which police armed with submachine guns mowed down a purse-snatcher from a helicopter.

more abstract types ("tale-types," from oral culture [Sullivan 183]), and "the journey toward the self ultimately includes and/or represents the journey toward the heart of the community" (184). In order for the characters to be able to function successfully, and by extension for the reader to be able to function successfully, within the community, the community's moral standards must be clearly, even spectacularly defined.[4] What might seem for an outside reader to be a heavy-handed, pedantic, sledgehammer approach to an ethical problem, therefore, is in fact a very provocative gauntlet thrown down to open up public debate. African writers are very much aware of their social responsibility, and they recognize that their readers expect to be enlightened, not just entertained. The novels of Andrew Sesinyi and Galesiti Baruti easily fit this pattern.

First, however, community identity must be defined, and one of the very first novels to do so for "Tswana" was written by a black South African. *Mhudi* is Sol Plaatje's fictionalized deliberation on the nature and consequences of colonial expansion into the interior of southern Africa. More recently, in *A Bewitched Crossroad*, Bessie Head wrote about similar problems during the period when Khama III (the Great) was consolidating his power in the face of threatened encroachments during the late nineteenth and early twentieth centuries. Both of these novels look at Tswana society in a period of rapid change and assess the way the society faces those changes. Although Plaatje is not technically a Botswana writer, his novel is included here because it opens up a discussion of how Botswana society has been represented and what it considers important about its own society.

*Mhudi* was written in 1917 as a contemplation of the changes that were taking place in South Africa at the time—land

---

4. See Njabulo Ndebele, *Rediscovery of the Ordinary*.

alienation, erosion of Africans' rights, and so forth. Plaatje set his novel during the disruptions caused in southern Africa by the Afrikaner Great Trek and Zulu expansion (*difaqane*). The novel is set in the 1830s and was written in 1917, shortly after the formation of the Union of South Africa in 1910, a time when the British actions in support of creation of the Union were seen as a betrayal by the Africans who had supported them during the South African (Anglo-Boer) war of 1899–1902. The Union government was proposing and passing laws that assigned where Africans could live; such legislation was designed to control a population that was seen as both a threat to the new nation and a source of cheap labor for the growing mining industry. In the 1830s, the time of *Mhudi*'s story, the enemies are the Matebele of Mzilikazi, who take without giving anything in return. The Matebele and Mzilikazi suffer a humiliating defeat at the hands of the allied BaRolong and Boers, and Plaatje suggests, in a speech by Mzilikazi to his people, that the new enemy (in 1917) will be the Boers:

> "[The Boers] will despoil them of the very lands they have rendered unsafe for us; they will entice the Bechuana youths to war and the chase, only to use them as pack-oxen; yea, they will refuse to share with them the spoils of victory....
>
> "[T]hey shall take Bechuana women to wife and, with them, breed a race of half man and half goblin, and they will deny them their legitimate lobolo." (154)

Mzilikazi's prediction about the future state of affairs would, of course, be clear to those reading the novel in the twentieth century. In 1917, at the time Plaatje was writing, the changes put into place by the government of the new Union of South Africa fulfilled his most dire predictions. The allies of the 1830s— the Boers—had become the new enemies of the 1910s. *Mhudi* leaves open the question about what will happen to the Boers, but the similarities in the two historical situations are made clear through the parallel structure.

The brutalities visited upon the Bechuana by the Matebele call for an answer, and Mzilikazi suffers that answer, just as Plaatje suggests that the white-controlled government will suffer for its crimes. But Mzilikazi represents a brutal, one-man system of rule, and Plaatje contrasts that style with the more consultative structures of BaRolong society: "Chief Moroka giving judgment said: 'Now you have all heard divers views on the marriage tangle before us. You have heard the views of old men; you have heard the views of younger men and the views of women too; you have heard the views of white men. And neither side can complain of having been ignored'" (107). The society of the Matebele, led by one dictator, seems too violent and thus too fragile to survive. The society of the BaRolong, one of the *merafe*[5] of the Batswana, contrasts with that of the Matebele as a strong society that will survive because of its more democratic, participatory nature. This novel offers perhaps one of the first instances of the "good" and just Tswana morality that is later praised in such works as *Love on the Rocks* and *Mr. Heartbreaker*. But unlike Sesinyi and Baruti, Plaatje does not ignore the changes taking place; neither is he blind to the injustices that exist within the society itself. His plea for equality

---

5. In precolonial Botswana, a *morafe* (plural *merafe*) was one of the independent kingdoms or chiefdoms into which the Tswana were divided. Their membership was usually composite and (especially in the north) could include large numbers of non-Tswana who were incorporated in varying degrees of subordination. The proto-states of the Tswana kings became Reserves under British rule, and the British translated *morafe* as "tribe," a translation that has caused some confusion, since for example the non-Tswana subjects of a Tswana chief could be described both as "members of his tribe" (his polity) and as "members of a different (subject) tribe." For more information, see Isaac Schapera, *The Ethnic Composition of Tswana Tribes*.

and fairness comes through in the depiction of and discussions by women.

Plaatje suggests that women represent the best hope for peaceful change and for bringing the best of the past into the present. Brian Willan in his biography of Sol Plaatje says of Plaatje's writing that "women, more than men, possessed the qualities from which a more just and humane society could emerge" (360). Shortly before Umnandi returns to Mzilikazi, she and Mhudi lament the lack of respect they receive in their societies:

> "How wretched," cried Mhudi sorrowfully, "that men, in whose counsels we have no share, should constantly wage war, drain women's eyes of tears and saturate the earth with God's best creation—the blood of the sons of women. What will convince them of the worthlessness of this game, I wonder?"
>
> "Nothing, my sister," moaned Umnandi with a sigh, "so long as there are two men left on earth I am afraid there will be war." (145)

By foregrounding the female characters Mhudi (for whom the novel is named), Hannetjie, and Umnandi and by characterizing them as good, strong, intelligent, and foresighted, Plaatje presents them as carriers of a better future, one without war (Umnandi and Mhudi) and without injustice (Hannetjie and Mhudi). Part of the problem, Plaatje suggests, is the result of the inferior status of women in all the societies concerned. Plaatje's vision is echoed in recent novels, where women also have an important part to play: Andrew Sesinyi, Mositi Torontle, and Unity Dow all see women as central to the processes of change in contemporary Botswana society, but in different ways. Unity Dow's novels will be dealt with in a later chapter.

Like *Mhudi*, Bessie Head's final novel, *A Bewitched Crossroad* (1984), is a historical novel, set during a period of significant

social and political transition in Botswana, and is therefore
discussed here briefly. Head's novel deals more explicitly with
Botswana; she sets the events in a ward of Khama's Bammang-
wato (or BaNgwato), against the period in the late nineteenth
century when land hunger was pushing British and Afrikaner
settlers further north. She intersperses chapters of historical
overview with chapters that look at the effects of the changes
from the perspective of one of the sub-chiefs, Sebina: "He was
the glorious representative of the past and tradition and yet he
hungered for the new and unknown" (63). Head here shows us
a man who acts as a bridge between the past and the future. He
is old, significantly, suggesting that although old ways change
and perhaps die out, they are to be respected. Sebina partic-
ipates in the changes that Khama brings to his society with
some trepidation, but also always believing that he has a role to
play. And the society does change, peacefully, because Khama
understands that change must be agreed upon and must offer
benefits. In Head's depiction of the people's discussion about
who will rule them, she identifies for the reader all the points
that must be considered by the people: "it was not a question
of his succeeding to the chieftainship of the Bamangwato but a
question of the new values he had acquired" (54). This practice
of consultation is an important feature of the society, as can be
seen already in *Mhudi*, and is a practice to which Khama continues to hold. On a matter of drawing boundaries of the new
Gamangwato Territory, Khama brings the issues to his *kgotla*,
and "[t]he matter was thrown open for public debate"; only
then can the decision be finalized:

> [Khama] ordered that a table and writing materials be
> brought into the courtyard as it was required that all the
> royal brothers and headmen of the town be witness to the
> document....
> Sebina was dazzled and blinded by the proceedings;

he knew not how he had moved forward nor how he re-
turned to his seat, except that all the generations and history he represented had suddenly met at that moment and
overwhelmed him. (119–20)

In passages such as these, Head makes clear the enormous capacity that exists in Tswana society for peaceful change, and
what that capacity relies on: Sebina, a man who had considered
himself too old for such things, finds himself fixing his signa-
ture, albeit with some younger help, to a document that helps
to establish the borders of the BamaNgwato Territory and the
future Botswana. Head's re-creation of Sebina shows us a model Botswana citizen. She shows readers how Botswana society
has changed and suggests that the tradition of peaceful change
was established quite early. The tradition continues right to the
present. Modern Botswana prides itself on its peaceful history. As we will see later, this peaceful tradition makes Botswana
appear uniquely appropriate for adventure novel and thriller
settings.

The tradition of peaceful change has its roots in part also
in the way Botswana was administered by the British. Because
of the way it was administered during the first half of the twentieth century, Bechuanaland did not suffer through many of
the problems, racial and other, that plagued and continue to
plague its neighbors. Since independence in 1966, Botswana
has enjoyed a stable democracy and a strong economy, thanks
to its large diamond deposits. Currently, however, Botswana is
undergoing another period of social change due in large part
to two factors: an increase in crime emanating from unemployment among school-leavers and a rising rate of HIV/AIDS in-
fections and deaths. Botswana society remains largely peaceful,
but people are having to cope with problems at a much faster
rate, and the difficulties in adjusting are the subject of much
modern Botswana literature.

The first major, postindependence piece of literature written in English by a Motswana is probably Andrew Sesinyi's *Love on the Rocks*, published in 1981 in Macmillan's Pacesetter series of popular romances. *Love on the Rocks* chronicles, rather predictably, the successful love story of Pule (from *pula*, meaning rain, as in prosperity; it is also the name of the Botswana currency as well as a shout of celebration), a boy from a rural family who runs away from a poor and abusive background, works his way through school, and finally wins a scholarship to the new University of Botswana.[6] There he meets Moradi (probably from *morwadi*, meaning daughter), a young girl from a more well-to-do family, a girl who has been raised in the new urban area of Gaborone, the country's capital. The novel deals with the "modernity versus tradition" culture clash on a number of levels, the central issue concerning Moradi's personal independence. According to tradition, the parents choose a husband for their daughter, but in *Love on the Rocks*, Moradi chooses love against her parents' wishes, and that love begets romantic violence when Patrick, the parents' choice for a husband, threatens and eventually beats up his rival Pule. The novel considers life in both urban and rural Botswana, describing the traditional way of life and the changes that a growing economy and urbanization bring to that way of life.

*Love on the Rocks* concludes formulaically in that everyone lives happily ever after. Here, all the major characters, and even more minor ones such as Patrick (the modern bad guy who drives a flashy car and is used to getting his way), reconcile themselves successfully to the events and the changes that they experience by calling upon tradition in a rather uncritical way. Pule's uncle, from whom Pule flees at the start of the

---

6. At the time Sesinyi was writing, the University would still have been the University of Botswana and Swaziland.

novel, stops drinking and becomes Pule's strongest supporter. Patrick finally accepts his defeat—quite gracefully—and sends Pule and Moradi a very expensive set of his-and-hers Rolex watches, being unable to shed the trappings and habits of his new, modern wealth. Moradi's father, after Pule appeals to his status as the patriarch of the traditional family, suddenly stops his abusive ways:

> Mr Baruti's movements were very swift for a man of his age. He turned back to Pule and at the same time struck out with an open hand at Pule's face. Moradi stifled a scream as the slap made a cracking sound on Pule's face. The two men stared at each other.
>
> Pule was the first to speak. "Papa! I have come to seek Moradi's hand in marriage."
>
> The furious look on Baruti's face lingered for a few seconds, and then his face fell. Moradi could hardly recognise her father. (140)

Once Pule calls Mr. Baruti "Papa" and reminds him of his paternal duties, Mr. Baruti stops his abusive ways and negotiates in good faith with Pule's family for the marriage to take place. By returning to the old values, the novel suggests, everything returns to its near-idyllic condition: "The two men stared at each other silently. Then Mr Baruti stood up, looking the boy straight in the face. 'I understand...I'm sorry,' Mr Baruti said" (141, ellipsis in original). By calling on more traditional relationships, this novel praises the traditional values of Tswana society. It presents an idealized picture of a people who can and do understand the need for change (and progressive change is a real feature of Botswana's "real" life). *Love on the Rocks* shows how a strong return to tradition can help people cope with modern life. Botswana is still the "good" country of Khama's times.

*Love on the Rocks* is still an extremely popular novel. Its concern with the problems of rural-urban migration, and its articulation of what is lost in moving to the city, continue to engage readers in Botswana. When a class of first-year students was asked to identify their favorite books, the two most popular were *Love on the Rocks* and the Setswana novel identified as *No Sweet without Sweat*. Both novels were said to give people good advice on how to live and to remind people of the importance of their tradition. *Love on the Rocks* is still in print twenty-five years later, but Sesinyi's second novel, *Rassie*, is not.

*Rassie* (1989, also published in Macmillan's Pacesetter series) opens with a tragic accident: a man and his pregnant wife are returning from a trip and hit an ox. They are killed, but the baby is saved and is raised by her uncle and aunt. The baby is called Rassie after the Afrikaans word *ras* (noise) because of the noise she makes crying while she is being cared for in the maternity ward of the hospital where her parents were taken. On the other side of the accident, the ox that the car hit was the prize ox owned by a man named Raseriri. He is quite proud of the beast, but his son Seriri, who was responsible for the ox, suffers from feelings of guilt because he feels responsible for the deaths of Rassie's parents. Rassie's uncle, who owns hundreds of cattle and takes care that they do not stray onto roads, decides that he must sue the owner of the ox that caused the accident, Raseriri, for damages caused by his beast, and Raseriri is financially ruined. Eventually, Mosweu, Raseriri's youngest son, decides to take revenge on the family he blames for his misfortune. He begins to stalk Rassie, whose uncle has become quite wealthy, while Mosweu's family slip even further into poverty.

This novel sets out the problems that arise in a country where there is such a big gap between the rich and poor. In this novel, Sesinyi gives a very direct treatment of rural poverty and oppression, one that is surprisingly un-idyllic, but his portrayal of the other more comfortable side of the picture perhaps shows the appeal of that kind of upper-middle-class lifestyle. *Rassie* also reflects a recognition of the difficulties cattle create in a society that values them so highly: wandering cattle do in fact constitute a serious road hazard, but reluctance to deal firmly with the danger they pose shows a certain contempt on the part of wealthy cattle owners for poorer families.[7]

*Rassie* opens with the luxury that Rassie's parents enjoy:

> The road raced back at them as the BMW Sedan sped towards the reddening horizon. The immense power of the three-litre engine was reassuringly audible as the couple travelling in the luxury car sat loose-limbed on the opulent sheepskin-covered seat. From the four stereo speakers—two at the rear and two at the front—music flowed soothingly. (1)

The power of the people in this car is unmistakable: the speed of the car, the sound of the powerful engine, the "opulent" seats, and no less than four stereo speakers, and the wife is even eating from a box of chocolates at her side—perhaps the definitive image of decadent, lazy wealth. The impression here, in addition to the one of power, is of people in a cocoon of comfort and safety, unaware of anything outside of their car, except for the road and the horizon, toward which they are heading. The ox that appears on the road in front of them is compared to a Minotaur (3), and the man is unable to stop the car because "[i]t was like using a string to stop an already-fired rocket" (3). The couple's sense of invulnerability is shattered by an almost mythic beast, one that might have come from Botswana's own mythology, and all the might of their wealth cannot help them in the face of this symbol of what Botswana society holds to be important. Cattle are everywhere, and Rassie's parents are sacrificial victims to Botswana's version of the Minotaur, a ritual

---

7. Newspapers publish periodic calls for the government to do something about stray cattle: the most drastic called for the Botswana Defence Force to patrol roads and shoot stray cattle on sight.

that demands many sacrifices, in fact: many people are killed in such accidents every year. The ox belongs to Raseriri, who is much less well off, and whose life is described as follows:

> Not far from the mangled mass of metal and once living creatures a much less privileged family existed in relative tranquility.
> Raseriri was a subsistence farmer and proud of it. He loved his small farm, his few goats, sheep and cattle....His family consisted of four boys, two girls and a hardworking, weather-beaten wife. The cattle-post-cum-farm was 40 kilometres away from the copper/nickel mining town of Selebi-Phikwe. By local standards, as a farmer, he was not worth a mention. (4)

Rassie's uncle is one of those men who can boast of hundreds of head of cattle, and the clash between the hardships faced by the Raseriri family and the greed of Rassie's uncle nearly has tragic consequences when Mosweu begins to stalk Rassie. In spite of the unhappy circumstances of the plot (rural poverty is depicted quite starkly), this novel has a positive outlook on contemporary Botswana society, as can be seen in the very first paragraph from the comfort and appeal of driving in a BMW. At the end of the novel, Rassie's uncle, terrified by what he and his desire for wealth cause to almost happen, uses his wealth "properly" to help the children of Raseriri's family. Rassie herself goes to school, thus demonstrating the belief—stated more clearly in *Love on the Rocks*—that education as well as respect for more traditional values and ways of life are keys to a successful modern life.

> Above [Rassie], a hawk floated in the clear skies, dived and soared up again with a tiny mouse in its claws. A dove cooed on a tree nearby, picking at insects for its breakfast. That was reality, a pleasant blend of life and death.
> The serenity of the young day was disturbed by the

sounds of civilisation. The day was ripe. Saturday was bursting into action. A large jet aircraft overflew the young people in its descent to the Gaborone airport. People came, people left. That was life. (135)

These final paragraphs present conflicting images of the natural and artificial worlds, but even here Sesinyi attempts to place them in a juxtaposition that does not lament the arrival of the modern world—reminding the readers once again of the seduction of the life to be had driving in a BMW—but rather he places them side by side, equally a part of life and death. The novel ultimately fails to resolve anything, however; Sesinyi presents a very interesting and complex picture of Botswana society, but succumbs to a kind of fairy-tale ending. Many characters die, but those who survive find happiness and prosperity. Perhaps tellingly, *Love on the Rocks* is still very popular; *Rassie* is no longer in print and extremely difficult to find.

*Rassie* gives a very uncomfortable portrayal of rural poverty and the consequences of the greed of people like Rassie's uncle. The novel also exposes the contradiction in Sesinyi's reclamation of Botswana morality. The comforts of technology, development, and the modern world are difficult, indeed impossible, to resist. But in spite of the desire to return to the old ways, if not the old physical reality, Sesinyi's novels seem unable to reconcile the convenience and seductiveness of the modern world with the morals that come with it. His characters all want the fast cars, the wealth, and the large, comfortable houses, but they are simultaneously unable to avoid the trap that wealth and material acquisition set for the unwary traditionalist. Sesinyi's third novel, *Carjack*, repeats many of the mistakes that are present in the first two novels of not questioning the entirety of the "development" package and in fact understanding it as a whole package, not something that can be interrogated and altered to suit the needs of the society.

*Carjack* was published in 1999. Sesinyi himself said that he wanted to write a cautionary tale about the dangers of crime ("crime doesn't pay"). The problems of new wealth and a loss of respect for traditional values are portrayed more starkly in this novel than in either *Love on the Rocks* or *Rassie*; however, two of the most striking points about this novel are first, the seductive portrayal of gangster life; and second, the prominence of powerful women.

*Carjack* takes a radically different view from its predecessors of change in Botswana society. Brutus, the protagonist, is a well-educated young man who lives with his grandmother and who enjoys the thrills and relatively easy money of his life of crime. The picture that is painted of this world, though, seems rather unrealistic. The employees of the syndicate are described predictably as "family people" with "kids to feed" (8); they are people who reject violence unless there is absolutely no alternative: "'We're not killers Brutus, my boy. We're business people....It's not so bad if you really think about it. Look, most expensive cars are insured, right? We don't take from the poor who have old beat-up cars that they can't insure'" (8). This is a kinder, gentler, carjacking syndicate that will use violence if forced to but is in fact thrown into some panic when Brutus becomes involved in murder. Not surprisingly, Brutus finds himself attracted to that life, and the rewards are not only monetary:

> For the next hour, Brutus experienced sexual activity he never thought could be so fulfilling. Every part of his body was explored and in turn, he was invited to do the same. In that hour, Brutus found the true definition of satisfaction.
>
> He was encouraged to be patient, made to build up to a satisfactory conclusion, guided to the peak of sensual pleasure and when the final moment came, he exploded into a billion sparks of ecstasy which left him satiated and

completely at peace with himself.

Brutus had had sexual experiences before, but nothing compared to his meeting with Mmapula Ditsamaiso—the Leader, for that was who she was. (54)

In this passage, it is difficult to read the situation as other than some kind of wish-fulfillment or gentle fantasy: everyone wants to be loved, and the soft tones of this passage describe erotic pleasure rather than brutal violence. Brutus is "encouraged to be patient" and is "completely at peace with himself." Such a description hardly matches the kind of environment one expects to find in Botswana's (or anyone's) underworld. The passage further confuses matters by dropping the bomb that this woman is the Leader of the Botswana arm of the carjacking syndicate.

Obviously, criminal bosses are not supposed to be female. Brutus himself nearly blows his first interview with her when he tries to act like a man:

"Don't you patronise me, you little ape," the woman hissed between clenched teeth. Her legs stood apart in a striking pose that enhanced her sexuality and her chest was heaving, but the stunned Brutus had had his hormones doused to wet ashes.

"Lesson number one," the Leader continued to hiss in a low but menacing tone. "When you work for me you store away whatever petty little thing makes you think you are the man before you come to see me." (32)

This passage mixes images of predatory pornography ("legs stood apart") with conventional images of romance ("her chest was heaving") with the additional conventional image of the angry woman as hissing cat. The confusion of what this woman is supposed to be leaves the reader with a strangely romanticized impression of the criminal underworld. In a sense, the world that Sesinyi creates is a combination of two "cultures" that collide here in Botswana: strong traditional women (albeit in a very strong patriarchy) in a society that is being fundamentally changed by the events and situations in what many Batswana see as a crime-ridden South Africa.

In this somewhat confused and symbolic way, the novel considers the emergence of powerful women into the public sphere. Sesinyi has worked as a civil servant, and he probably observed the rise of powerful women around him. There are currently a number of powerful members of parliament and ministers who are women, and the women's rights organization *Emang Basadi* remains strong—in the face of continued gender inequality—fifteen years after being founded. So although people speak of their mothers and grandmothers with a kind of reverence, as does *Carjack*'s Brutus, Botswana has only recently begun to see women in public positions of power. *Carjack* translates this trend into popular fiction, in a simultaneously surprising and predictable way.

In *Mhudi*, the three most brave, sensible, and intelligent people are women: Mhudi, Hannetjie, and Umnandi. In *Carjack*, the two most powerful and evil gangsters are women—and they are extremely powerful and predatory—one is the Leader of the Botswana division of the South African carjacking syndicate, and the other is the organization's financial wizard. There are two important aspects of this constellation. First of all, women are in charge, a reflection no doubt of the changing dynamics of power in Botswana society. The "old boys' network" no longer functions in the way that it used to, for example in the *kgotla* or even in the relationship between Pule and Moradi's father in *Love on the Rocks*. These women in Sesinyi's fictional world are completely in control of what happens in their territory (although not in control of the orders that come from the big bosses in South Africa, possibly reflecting the popular perception that all major crime comes from South Africa). But unlike Mhudi and Umnandi, for example, these two women are very obviously criminals, not admirable gender rebels. The Leader and the financial Donna are evil, creepy, and dangerous. In "real life," most powerful criminals are not women, but Sesinyi creates his most powerful and evil "bad guys" in the mold of female sexual predators.

The gender-role implications of these characters are intriguing. In the end, all the bad guys get bumped off, but only some of the bad girls do. The organization is still run by a woman: the financial wizard takes over after the glamorous but evil Leader is killed along with Brutus (who has been corrupted by the evil Leader) and the beautiful, good, but boring Boitumelo (Brutus's girlfriend). The more traditional female, in the person of Brutus's grandmother, disappears completely from the setting of the novel even before the halfway point. Brutus lives in fear that his grandmother will find out about and suffer (emotionally and otherwise) on account of his life as a carjacker, but her influence—and the influence of all such women—wanes in the face of the threat from the new modern female as well as the threat from murder-infested South Africa. The world in *Carjack* has changed so much that a return to the old morals is in fact virtually impossible. Plaatje praises the influence of such strong women. At the end of *Mhudi*, Ra-Thaga promises his wife that "'from henceforth, I shall have no ears for the call of war or the chase; my ears shall be open to one call only besides the call of the chief, namely the call of your voice—Mhudi'" (165). Sesinyi's confused message reflects perhaps a confusion about the place of men and women in this new and changing society.

The suggestion of danger in the way women have risen to power is interesting and somewhat disturbing. Sesinyi's novel does not so much critique the ethics or morals of a society in which violent crime is on the rise, but it reveals instead a patriarchal fear of strong women in public places, of women in charge. In both *Love on the Rocks* and *Rassie*, the plot complications sort themselves out when the male heads of households (Pule's uncle, Moradi's father, and Rassie's uncle) return to the values that put them in charge: appropriately arranged marriages, proper respect for parents and proper responsibility from elders, accountable wealth, and so forth. In *Carjack*, such an option is not available; first, because there is another evil woman to step in and fill the vacuum that the Leader's death opens up; and second, because the world of *Carjack* is not a good—that is, moral—world. Botswana is a good place, with solid Botswana values; South Africa is a bad place, where crime comes from. Johannesburg's underworld is superimposed on Gaborone, and thus society no longer makes sense in a traditional context. Women as mothers and wives can be strong and even fearsome as long as they do not step outside their traditional places in the society.

Galesiti Baruti's novel *Mr. Heartbreaker* (1993) considers these changes in Botswana society in a much more lurid, colorfully written, and less confused way. The story concerns a young man, Robi Marae, and the trail of broken hearts (and bodies) he leaves behind in the fast-paced social whirl of Gaborone, also known as "Gabs." Baruti also wants to write a moral novel, but unlike Sesinyi, he does not lose sight of his project in the realm of fantasies of sexual satisfaction. Baruti's prose is bombastic and entertaining, but his point is never lost; Gabs is a repulsive place. Consider the following passage:

> [Robi's] girl was the youngest. He hunched over the poor little thing with his tall body. It was like a thirsty giraffe of the Kalahari Central Game Reserve hunching over a very small watering hole. Like a watering hole scared to lose all it's [sic] little water, the school girl cringed as if to disappear from the face of the earth. This was a classic case of dirty defilement. Any loving parent who saw this would die right away....The poor little thing turned away its shivering cold face as Robi put his bearded mouth down

on her for a romantic kiss. That romantic feeling melted away when the mouth missed that little inexperienced mouth by many inches. Robi tried again and this time the romance in his mouth melted into the hair in the center of the little girl's head. With anger swelling in his nerves Robi placed his hands around the girl's head and tilted it upwards. He placed his mouth on that of the girl and extended his sour tasting tongue out towards the inside of the girl's mouth.

The little girl whimpered a little at the rough manner in which her head was tilted up....The tongue was rich with the taste of the cold beers and the heavily spiced roasted meat. But, to the little girl, the taste was like that of a poison from that mamba which nearly killed her grandfather at the cattlepost some years back. Should she scream and run away? No she would never dream of that. For the simple reason that she wanted to have a lot of news for her friends who were unlucky never to have had a brush with the mighty Groovers. (161)

Despite the confusion of images that Baruti uses, he gives us a very clear picture of a near-rape (the event never ultimately occurs, in part because Robi is stabbed to death and has his nose cut off before anything happens). Baruti does not absolve the schoolgirl from her complicity in her situation—indeed, we are warned at the beginning of the novel "'Do not be bluffed by those clean and well-ironed school uniforms...'" (5)—but any pleasure to be derived from the situation is removed by the images of the sour-tasting tongue and the poison of the deadly mamba—adding a note of irony, as well, to the thrill of "a brush with the mighty Groovers." There is no way out for these characters, or for anyone in this novel; the number and manner of deaths of most of the leading characters is astonishing. The language is idiosyncratic, extravagant, and unorthodox, and the novel is remarkably effective (and a fun read); nevertheless, the moral about the importance of good old Botswana values remains intact.

Recent writing by women seems to offer a critical alternative and also a more positive approach to the problem of change and to the frightening future that writers like Sesinyi and Baruti envision. As noted earlier in this chapter, much of the criticism of contemporary society and of the way more traditional values are applied to that society comes from contemporary women writers such as Unity Dow and Mositi Torontle. Torontle's *The Victims*, published in 1993, deals with issues of generational conflict and change in a more focused way than Sesinyi. The structure of *The Victims* also employs a similar parallel format to *Mhudi*, making use of the same characteristic resonance between different time periods to show continuity but also to call attention to aspects of society that ought to change further: most specifically, the belief that not everything that comes with traditional ways is good for everyone.

*The Victims*, the first (and so far, only) novel by Torontle, tells the story of one period in a young girl's life and is a novel particularly of rural life and rural poverty. Dineo ("gifts") is working hard to do well at school, and her mother makes numerous sacrifices so that her daughter can get an education. Dineo's father went to work in the mines in South Africa when Dineo was a child, leaving the mother to fend for herself. Their situation was a common one in the 1970s and 1980s. It presents the problems that girls face when they are in school, but it also places the problems in the context of the political climate in southern Africa in the 1980s, when South Africa was still an apartheid state, and families were broken apart because of the labor needs of the South African mines. Dineo's boyfriend, Tom, is a journalist from South Africa, and their relationship, like countless others at the time, suffers from the strains created by the life of exiles and migrants.

*The Victims* is an engaging novel, and compares in many

interesting ways with its predecessors by Sesinyi and Baruti, as well as with novels about Botswana by non-Batswana—in particular with respect to descriptions of the land and the bush. About the day of the school agricultural fair, for example, Torontle writes, "This morning, the 14th of May 1979, was a historic day in her life....Consequently, Dineo had ironed her uniform until every crease was straightened" (5). Baruti's warnings about the dire prospects represented by schoolgirls in their well-ironed uniforms do not fit here, because Dineo is preparing for an important school event.

The most significant educational event is, of course, the final-year set of examinations, which determine who may continue with school. The exams make us understand the role of education in helping pupils understand Botswana society. During the history exam, for example, students are asked not only to describe historical events, but also to place them in the context of the society that Botswana has become:

> The sound of scribbling pens raised a silent scream as the students desperately tried to defeat the time limit....One of the compulsory questions was: "Either 'Reconstruct the conversation Kgosi Sechele had with missionaries when he discovered that Solomon, a man after God's heart, had many wives and concubines' or 'define the significance of Kgosi Sechele's defence of traditional doctors among early missionaries for our current world.'" (50)

The questions that pupils are being asked to consider neither require them to praise the old ways and denigrate the new ones, nor vice versa, but rather to understand the processes and debates that have led to the construction of current beliefs. Education here is a kind of bridge between the way things used to be done and the way things are understood now. This representation of education prepares the pupils—and readers, of course—for the critical tone of the later parts of the novel.

A further comparison can be made with attitudes toward the land that appear in novels by non-Batswana. In *The Victims*, the land is a much more friendly place than it is almost anywhere else in Botswana literature. Here, for example, we read about Dineo's love for the garden:

> The garden work got off the ground and produced wonderful vegetables....The rich river bank soil graciously nourished the plants. Dineo fell in love with the damp garden soil and everything in it. With her own hands she tendered [sic] the plants with great love and care. Apart from the classroom and their humble home, the garden became her favourite place. (14)

Torontle's portrait of the land is much more gentle—gracious—than the hostile portrait that comes out in much other writing. The loving, familial relationship is spelled out later, when the students are learning to sing the national anthem. Their choirmaster takes them outside the school grounds to really see what they are singing about[8]:

> "The moment was religiously serene and demanded reverent seeing. We bent half way, peeped through the thick air and we began to see through his eyes. We turned, slowly, and saw the furthest point, down there, where the earth and the horizon kissed, where some blue meandering mountains lilted across the land, so lost and unknown to us, but they smiled and cried with us. Then we looked all over turning around, slowly, following his gestures. We began to look to the West where the tall eucalyptus trees of our school swayed at a distance. And then slowly,

---

8. The particular lines from the national anthem comprise the first verse:
*Fatshe leno la rona,*
*Ke mpho ya Modimo,*
*Ke boswa jwa borraetsho;*
*A le nne ka kagiso.*

we tamed our stretching sight, back to focus on the very ground under our feet." (66)

The spiritual nature of the people's relationship to their land—and of the land's relationship to its people—is obvious from the first sentence: people worship and revere the place where they live. The relationship between the pupils and what they see is made clear to them by their teacher, who asks them to look literally around them: what they finally see and understand is not just some pretty landscape, but a line of mountains that cries with them, the land that is, through the circling motion of their view, connected to their own feet, the same land that "graciously" provides vegetables for Dineo and her family to eat. Later, Dineo teaches Tom about the dangers of the *mophane* forest: "'The spirits of the *mophane* trees are too friendly. They like human company. If they hear one's name they can keep on calling you into the deeper forest until one gets completely lost and never returns home'" (65). Of course, the bush is always dangerous: it is a place of wild animals, witchcraft, and other threats to human life and society, but it is also beloved, and the friendly attitude of the trees here bears hardly any relation to the hostile and dangerous environment described by writers such as Butler, Rush, and others.

*The Victims* is set up in three parts; the first two parallel one another in the stories of the mother and the daughter. The first part concerns the story of how Dineo's mother married Dineo's father and how the father abandoned them when he left to work in the mines in South Africa; the second part concerns the mother's desire that the daughter be educated and not repeat

---

(Blessed be this noble land,
Gift to us from God's strong hand,
Heritage our fathers left to us,
May it always be at peace. [*Macmillan Social Studies Atlas for Botswana* 1])

48

her own mistakes, but it also chronicles the relationship between Dineo and Tom, her boyfriend; the third part gives a resolution to the situation that arises between Dineo and Tom (they are siblings who are unaware of their relationship[9]). This resolution is interesting because it offers a "way out" for the man who leaves Dineo, a way not available to Dineo's father, but it also brings warnings from the mother about the importance of education and the dangers of running around with men:

> "Time has arrived for you to resume your journey." Dineo looked down ashamed that she ever paused from her studies. "I still have full confidence in your morality, competence, and capabilities. The fact that you slipped along the way, has nothing to do with you but the very road we tread. I know you are a brilliant girl," she said emphatically.
>
> "Thank you, Mum, for believing in me and for this second chance."
>
> "Only remember this," Mmapula said, touching her daughter tenderly on the shoulder…."Only remember," she repeated, "no man is different. Any man can make you pregnant and desert you. Forget about them until you are in a position of strength, that is, when you are educated enough to stand on your own if need be." (123)

Mmapula is not unlike Head's Sebina, a representative of tradition but eager to see change come to her life in the figure of her daughter. Mmapula's morality—or at least the morality she understands her daughter to possess—incorporates a strong sense of self-protection and autonomy. Dineo, like her mother, allows "love" to get in the way of her dreams, but unlike her mother, does not allow the consequences of that love to prevent

---

9. There is an interesting parallel here to Bessie Head's *The Cardinals*, although Torontle was probably not familiar with Head's first novel.

her from following them altogether. Both Dineo and her mother recall the women of *Mhudi*, who lament the narrow social perceptions of a woman's place in the community as mothers and laborers. For Dineo and Mmapula, those two identities are still important, but they want to be equal partners to men.

Torontle's work (along with Unity Dow's) seems to represent the beginnings of a new era of Botswana literature. Recent writing by women offers more of a challenge to "the way things are" and have been. Male writers still want an ending or a lesson that reflects Khama's moral legacy, but their sense of morality is becoming confused, as can be seen in Sesinyi's *Carjack*. In a society that is changing rapidly, the literature by men seems to cope with changes by calling more strongly for a return to the old ways, while that by women seems to respectfully question some of those same old ways, as well as the new ones. Dineo, although strongly attached to her mother and to her home, looks to Western education specifically as a way to strengthen her position (and by extension, that of all women) in a society that favors men.

More recent women's writing (especially poetry and short stories) explores issues of forced or arranged marriage, *bogadi*,[10] domestic violence, and so on, and seems to be moving away

---

10. *Bogadi* (also *lobola*) refers to the transfer of property (normally cattle) made from the bridegroom's family to the bride's, which legitimates marriage and defines the status of any children. The payment of *bogadi* is what (classically) defined a relationship as a legitimate marriage, in which the woman and, crucially, her children belonged to the husband's family. If no *bogadi* was paid, the relationship would be illegitimate and the children would belong to the mother's family. Anthropologists have seen the transaction as a compensation for the woman's labor and reproductive capacity (labor and population, rather than land, being the crucially scarce resources in premodern southern Africa). Missionaries criticized *bogadi* as purchase of women, and some chiefs were induced to abolish or discourage it, but now it has again become standard.

from the prescriptive tendency represented by Sesinyi and Baruti. The work of these new writers signals perhaps a shift to a more critical literature, one that does not reject Tswana-ness (however they define that Tswana-ness) but also interrogates how the tradition and society will adapt to new ways of understanding the world—how to preserve what is "exceptional" without sacrificing what is "Bo-Tswana."

# "LITERARY" NOVELS OF BOTSWANA

The previous chapter looked at novels that describe how Batswana see themselves, looking at how they see their society and what they think is wrong with it, and what they think is strong in their society. This chapter deals with novels that look at Botswana, that aspire to receive more "serious" critical attention than do the other genres of novels, such as detective and adventure. Alexander McCall Smith's Precious Ramotswe novels have received a great deal of attention, but they will be discussed in a separate chapter. Adventure novels as a genre have of course also been studied, but the next chapter will examine them. With the exception of Norman Rush and possibly Naomi Mitchison, the writers of the novels discussed here have not been widely circulated or studied and are probably not very familiar.

These novels are set in the place Botswana, and although Botswana seems to be an important aspect of the novels, ultimately, they are often only tangentially about it. Each writer wants to capture something about Botswana, but they are only successful in that endeavor insofar as they are able to write in more than a superficial fashion about the people of the country. For most writers, including Norman Rush, Botswana—at first an interesting place with a fascinating desert landscape and an unusual history—is really only a place to figure out one's place in the world at large. An important exception to this pattern is Naomi Mitchison, whose novel *When We Become Men* focuses almost entirely on the relationships and intrigues of village, political, and refugee life in Bechuanaland in the early 1960s.

The discussion that follows will show that the protagonists must fight with the landscape (in this case, the Kalahari Desert) in order to gain self-knowledge, not knowledge about Botswana and the Batswana. In Botswana, in order to get the self-knowledge that is the presumed destiny of every white person who comes to Africa, one must conquer—or at least survive—the desert. These novels illustrate the classic "man versus nature" plot and conflict, in which the test of the self is played out against a harsh environment. The fact that other people live in that same environment and "conquer" it regularly is irrelevant to the central quest, as it is irrelevant to the adventure genre, as discussed in the next chapter.

However, Naomi Mitchison proves the exception to the rule. *When We Become Men* was originally published in 1965. Mitchison's knowledge of Tswana society undoubtedly came from her long association (from 1960 until her death) with the BaKgatla and their Paramount Chief Linchwe, although *When We Become Men* must have been written early in that relationship. Her ties with Linchwe led to her being made the adoptive mother of both the Chief and the BaKgatla, and her association with them produced a number of writings, including children's stories about the BaKgatla as well as more historical pieces about Botswana's culture and traditions. *When We Become Men* is her only novel for adults set in Botswana.

In this novel, Mitchison resists playing the anthropologist cataloguing the characteristics of the Batswana, unlike Norman Rush's narrator in *Mating*. *When We Become Men* is not a descriptive portrait of Botswana and does not pretend to offer information about "how we lived in the past"; instead, it explores the problems that faced young Batswana in the early 1960s, presumably the problems that Linchwe himself faced as the British-educated heir to the paramount chieftainship of one of Botswana's major *merafe*. *When We Become Men* interrogates these problems of colonial administration, missionary education, and strong traditions by exploring the dynamics of the relationships between a number of characters.

*When We Become Men* begins with a question: "One of them was asleep—was he?" (9). The answer to this question determines where Isaac, the protagonist, will—literally—land. He is on a train headed south from Francistown; he has been arrested in Rhodesia and is being deported back to South Africa through Bechuanaland, when he takes the opportunity of his guards' sleep and distraction to jump off the train into the bush. Isaac does not know much about Bechuanaland, but fears that

> [h]e must be in the middle of nowhere, tribal country, but he didn't even know which tribe. That wasn't the kind of thing they'd ever thought about. Everything that mattered for Africa was happening in the towns. Some of his friends had said that these tribal people were against them, hated them, would give them up to the Special Branch, being well paid for it. (11)

For Isaac, the "problem" of Botswana is that it is rural and "tribal": unlike in the other novels considered in this chapter, what has to be overcome here is not the bush but a very familiar human resistance to change and to new ideas. The traditions that are practiced and upheld by the people whom Isaac is about to ask for refuge are holding them back; Africa's future lies "in the towns," in modern life. Isaac spends his first few hours of freedom worrying about who will pick him up, trying to identify the greater evil: the "tribal people," the police, or even the South African Special Branch (who are known to have agents in Bechuanaland).

However, once Isaac and his friend Josh (with whom he was arrested and who also escapes after his arrest) arrive in the village of Ditlabeng, capital of the Bamatsieng,[1] they are forced to see this life in a new way. The old chief is persuaded by the white District Commissioner to allow the refugees to stay because "'if people are going to be killed or tortured or put into concentration camps, you have to help them'" (19), and he is persuaded in spite of the opposition of his nephew. Isaac and Josh are given a place to stay and begin to get odd jobs repairing radios and other devices. They also get glimpses into the complicated politics of the village.

In the period before independence, political parties began to organize themselves, and in *When We Become Men* these competing ideologies have representatives in many of the characters. The young chief, Letlotse, wishes to abdicate his chieftainship in order to form a leftist political party; he is supported by his cousin Motswasele but opposed by his male relatives, who want him to call up an age regiment and become initiated into manhood according to tradition. Motswasele is appointed regent for Letlotse after the old chief dies (and while Letlotse is still studying in England), but he has political ambitions of his own, including retaining the chieftainship after Letlotse returns from England. For Isaac and Josh, this battle between Letlotse

---

1. Literally, people of Matsieng. Matsieng is a mythical figure who is said to have emerged from the rocks near Mochudi, the capital of the BaKgatla. Matsieng is sometimes considered the ancestor of all Batswana. The name Bamatsieng is fictional, although the reference to the BaKgatla is clear.

and Motswasele is particularly important: Motswasele would like to sell them to the Special Branch agents, but Letlotse becomes their friend. As a demonstration of their loyalty to the Bamatsieng, both join age regiments and are ritually initiated into Bamatsieng cultural and social manhood.

With this constellation of characters, Mitchison demonstrates both the modernity of traditional customs and the prejudice of modern ways. Isaac is not only swept up in the intrigues surrounding the succession to the chieftainship, he is also involved with a group of exiled South African resistance fighters operating in a nearby town. When this group is infiltrated by an informer, Isaac does not recognize the man as a traitor, and his eagerness to return to important resistance work nearly costs the members of his group their freedom. The parallel intrigues in the traditional village and the modern town demonstrate the modernity of traditional relationships as well as the traditional aspects of modern ones.

Mitchison does not present her readers with a simple choice of good versus evil or modern versus tradition, however. As the plot unfolds, the intrigues appear more and more entangled, and nothing is as simple as a choice between binaries. None of the characters embodies these contradictions more than Isaac himself. He is an utterly "modern African," who disdains the prejudices and superstitions of the old way of life, but who finds that his life depends on the good will of that way of life. When the chief grants him and Josh permission to stay in Ditlabeng, Isaac suddenly finds himself "kneel[ing] on the floor, on the lion skin, and giv[ing] thanks to their chief with due respect. Almost with love" (25). This modern man then demonstrates his respect for his new chief by repeatedly, and without charging him, repairing the tuning knob on the chief's radio, when he knows that the radio will come back once "old Ham hand the chief" gets annoyed and pulls the knob off again. He recognizes as he repairs the radio that he has "more respect [for the chief] than he'd ever had for anyone: even the head of the [resistance] group whose name they never even knew" (26). Through the rest of the novel, Isaac longs for both his "old" resistance work and also his "new" people.

From the very beginning of *When We Become Men*, the bush is not the enemy. The enemy is isolation and not knowing who your people are. In a discussion with Letlotse about the possibility of being what he calls a "civilized chief," Isaac states emphatically that he accepts Letlotse as his chief:

> "Remember there was a time when I thought that all this about tribes and chiefs was nonsense, was wrong, was taking us back into the bad past, as surely as Verwoerd and Vorster would put us there. I thought a tribe was utterly against progress. Against freedom and democracy. As they try to make them in the Republic. In the Bantustans. I thought it was another kind of slavery."
>
> "And now you think—?" said Letlotse softly.
>
> Isaac's hand gripped the edge of the bench; the sun was almost down now and in the longer, softer shadow that stretched right across the *lapa*, you could see the small pale flames of the stick fire that shows there is life in the house. "What I think now is harder to say," said Isaac. "Because I do not believe it has been said before. But it could be that our tribes are the kind of coming together, the kind of society, which we all want in our hearts. Not always, perhaps, but now, this month, among your people, the Bamatsieng, who are my people also, while every man and woman is in a common purpose. And the purpose is you, Letlotse, you, the heir, the chosen one. And you have to act so that this common purpose is worth the whole of life." (225)

Isaac begins to recognize at this point that what is worth preserving about "tribal life"—"the common purpose" that "is worth the whole of life"—is also what he wants to fight for in the resistance against the apartheid society of South Africa. This common purpose is identified and affirmed by a white man who argues for refuge; it is reinforced when Isaac accepts the Bamatsieng as his people in his marriage to Tselane, and it is confirmed when he accepts his place in the new chief's regiment. His fight in South Africa will have new meaning for him precisely because he has people—particular people, the Bamatsieng, and a family with Tselane—from whom he has learned and for whom he is fighting. As he considers whether to return to South Africa, he thinks about

> the moral order and how here in Bechuanaland it could be entirely an order for peace and prosperity, for progress and education and happiness. But back in the Republic it could be none of these things. It was still an order of fighting and perhaps, before one could think of such things as happiness, one had to think of courage and steadfastness, the virtues of war, of the old moral order of the tribes. (229)

The new moral order for which Isaac fights does not spring from a vacuum. It is "still an order of fighting": "still" not only in the context of South Africa, where civil rights have not been extended to all citizens, but also "still" in the context of the village, where groups with allegiances to different men fight for power. The virtues of "courage and steadfastness" are not so old and outdated after all.

The choice for Isaac and Letlotse—indeed for all the characters—is the same, but each chooses a different path to participation in the community. *When We Become Men* speculates about the choice facing a modern African nation, and Mitchison's portrayal of the inner conflicts that must be part of choosing draws the reader's attention to the commonalities, the differences, and the benefits that contribute to making the choice itself ultimately impossible. For Letlotse, a traditional chief with a modern education, the choice cannot be absolute—either this or that—but must encompass compromise and embrace both change and constancy.

Mitchison writes with sympathy of this dilemma, and *When We Become Men* succeeds exactly because it addresses questions of the human spirit, and not questions of the (white) individual's search for personal meaning in a hostile physical environment. The novel does demonstrate some flaws[2] that are perhaps characteristic of the period during which she wrote, but in spite of these, *When We Become Men* is a refreshing read—a kind of thoughtful speculation from the outside about what life might be like for a people facing great challenges.

Carolyn Slaughter is a writer who spent part of her childhood in Botswana and who as a child became attached to the Kalahari Desert, a place of escape from her abusive father, a colonial official in the Bechuanaland Protectorate. She has written a number of other novels as well as a memoir of her childhood in Botswana, *Before the Knife* (London: Black Swan Books, 2002). *Dreams of the Kalahari* is organized into a number of parts that seem at times unrelated, but this aspect of the structure might simply reflect the hesitations of a very young novelist. Both the structure and the content of Slaughter's novel are reminiscent of Doris Lessing's cycle *The Children of Violence*, which traces the life of Martha Quest in Rhodesia. *Martha Quest* opens, too,

---

2. For example, the stilted attempt to represent Setswana in English. Characters who are apparently speaking Setswana to each other simply sound uneducated. When Tselane explains to Isaac how the traitor's children came to their house, she says, "'Meant to take you all into his trap, then meant to come back himself, money in pocket, thirty pieces silver, more. Meant he'd settle here, get his kids over. The mother dead, see. Meant to get them educated here'" (151). Although readers are probably meant to recognize that the characters are not speaking in English, it is not clear why Setswana should like be made to resemble incorrect English.

with a young girl sitting under a tree (reading Havelock Ellis), and subsequent novels in the cycle deal with Martha's gradual sexual awakening, her move away from home, and then her migration from Rhodesia to London. Up to that point, Slaughter's protagonist, Emily, follows a similar path.

*Dreams of the Kalahari* (1981) begins in the Bechuanaland Protectorate, before independence. The protagonist Emily, like the writer, is the daughter of a colonial official, a veterinary inspector. This fact has important implications for Emily: class relations among whites in the Bechuanaland Protectorate were such that, had Emily's father been a missionary, a settler farmer, or an administrative officer, she might not have been so isolated. Emily's mother longs for England, and Emily escapes regularly to the bush to get away from the oppressive atmosphere at home. Eventually, she moves back to England, but realizes that she is not happy there and that Botswana is, in fact, more "home" to her than any place else.

*Dreams of the Kalahari* opens like this: "The small girl sat on the sand under a thorn tree" (9). This is Botswana, so not surprisingly we find ourselves in the desert, with thorn trees. The small girl is there, but she is alone, and she is white. *Dreams of the Kalahari* is a *Bildungsroman*, and what is noteworthy throughout the novel about this growing up is Emily's need—both psychological and physical—for the landscape of the Botswana desert, captured in the following three examples from different points in the novel:

> The gray Kalahari sand spread itself wearily towards the pink line of the horizon; Emily thought of this as a mouth that swallowed the sun at the day's end. She did not want to see it happen… (3).

> Over the next five years spent in the school Emily was to pine for the bush (120).

> "I want to stay here for ever, and never, never move. I

want to grow into this place, grow old and be put in the ground like the Africans and come up as a tree. I want to be dug deep into it till my bones rot and turn to powder" (177).

These examples show the importance of the bush in Emily's development, but they also show the development of her relationship to Botswana. The first description of the desert bush attributes a weariness, a tiredness to the bush, exposing an anxiety about the loss of something—the day? a way of life?—that does not hint at the sense of rejuvenation that comes later, when Emily sees the possibility for renewal even in death. Here Emily begins to see that the land has something to offer that others have been using, and she alludes to the link that she later clearly identifies (she wants to "grow into this place" and to be buried "like the Africans") between the land and those who live there.

Within the novel, Emily's need to be in Botswana is placed in sharp contrast to her parents' desire to go Home (capital H)[3] to England and to the Africans' "need" for land. Her mother tells her, "'You're an English girl. England is your home. You should be proud'" (138). The imagery of the land is here used quite conventionally: according to her mother, Emily's attachment to the desert must be imagined, since she is not a part of it. The Africans do not see the bush the same way as Emily; the bush is a place of danger, and safety is represented by the society of other human beings. Emily's attachment is necessarily different because she goes to the bush in order to *escape* the people around her.

---

3. The term "Home" was used by British expatriates and settlers throughout the empire and carries a range of complex connotations beyond those of home in the simple or literal meaning. In this example, the usage emphasizes the contrast between Emily's and her parents' sense of where they belong.

At first, however, Emily wants to be alone, and her emotional life is tied to what she understands to be the solitude of the desert. It is important that Emily's landscape be empty; for her self-development and self-identity, it must be an uninhabited wilderness because only in an uninhabited place can she discover herself and define herself without reference to other people. She goes into the bush to feel alive and safe, with no other people around. Even though Emily interacts with the Batswana in her other environment at the house, she is clearly different from them. She hears stories, visits them at home and in the village, and incorporates what she learns from them into her outlook, but for much of the novel, they remain very much part of the background, and the bush remains empty.

Ironically, Emily's emotional life does come to rely on Africans themselves, but not until she moves away from Bechuanaland to London.[4] While she is in London, she becomes involved in the antiapartheid activities that swept up British people as well as southern Africans living abroad,[5] and so the people of southern Africa become part of the cause that gives her life added meaning. While she is in London, she reestablishes contact with a school friend, Virginia, and makes friends among the South African exiles there. Then she has a dream about the bush: "'Virginia, last night I dreamt that I was home again. I dreamt I was walking far out into the bush, and coming towards me was a whole lot of people, walking quietly, and I was going to join them, I didn't know what for. But I was so happy,

---

4. At this point, the similarities between Emily's and Martha Quest's paths end. Martha Quest's life becomes part of a postnuclear future, and her death is only vaguely referred to.

5. A number of white South Africans (and residents of the Bechuanaland Protectorate) were able to move easily to England because they were able to retain their British passports while they were also citizens of South Africa.

Virginia'" (200). This dream uses what is for Emily a familiar image: comfort and safety in the bush, only this time, she is going to join "a whole lot of people," *and* they made her "so happy."

Emily returns to Botswana and finds peace in a refugee camp that is under siege from the hostile forces operating over the borders in South Africa, Angola, and Zimbabwe. Slaughter's fictional vision of Botswana is somewhat different from the way events actually played themselves out, but at the time, such a vision would undoubtedly have seemed reasonable, given the number of conflicts in the region. And still, Botswana here is a kind of nonracial paradise[6] that exists in direct opposition to South Africa, and here, Emily discovers a landscape that is very heavily populated. The refugee camp she works in provides the focus as a community center for a number of villages in the vicinity, and people appear out of the surrounding bush, as in her dream, as if out of nowhere: "They did not stop work until just before dark; then people began to disappear back into the bush, trailing or carrying their treated children" (243). This bush is no longer the unoccupied solitude of Emily's childhood:

> In the bush, just beyond the huts, she could hear the crickets and seemed to feel the presence of African ancestors, protecting and watching over the land....
>
> She looked away to all the little fires winking at the entrances of huts. The African life was in full swing now, with laughter and shouting and endless complaints about the beer which had run out. A woman was singing a soft rippling song, accompanied by a drum and hosho rattle. Farther away, a five-stringed lute trickled out an independent melody and a bow blended in with the other melodies so that they became a haunting intricate whole. (245–46)

---

6. This image echoes Botswana's own ideal of itself: the flag depicts the blue (background) of the sky that welcomes both white and black (central stripes) under its umbrella; in addition, the national symbol is the zebra.

The language of this passage is telling. Emily acknowledges the existence of the ancestors in the land, but she turns away from it (after all, they are not really her ancestors) and from the bush to the life that is going on in the huts and in the camp more generally, which she perceives as "a haunting intricate whole." Her attachment to the landscape remains, but it is superseded by her growing attachment to the people who in fact live there, and have lived there for a long time.

Emily's attachment is symbolized most specifically by her adoption of the Angolan orphan baby Happy. She is at first reluctant to take on this new responsibility, much as she was unable to cope with the people: Emily "was about to be firm, not to allow herself to be manipulated. But the wretched child had nestled against her and fallen asleep" (239). Later, her co-worker asks her where she got the baby: "'I haven't exactly got it,' Emily said snappishly…" (241). Finally, she gives in to her affection for the baby:

> Earlier, Lala had come and taken the baby from Emily. "She go now for her feeding, and she sleep next to Mattie's baby. She like that. How about we call her Happy? Because she never cry. Okay with you, Emily? You happy now too. I bring her back in the morning for you."
>
> Emily had agreed to this arrangement; she'd very quickly grown fond of the baby, who gurgled and chuckled and fastened herself around her fingers. (245)

Emily's resistance to emotional—human—attachment, as she comes to learn, cannot be divorced from her emotional attachment to the land. This is what she must learn if she is to live successfully in Africa—in Botswana. Emily wants at first only the solitude of the land, but not the company that comes with it. In London, she gets to know the people, even as she is separated from the country. As Emily comes to accept Happy, the baby, she also comes to accept her place with the people, not just on the land. The significance of the baby's name for Emily herself is never actually commented on in the novel, but the implications for Emily's own happiness of accepting Happy are clear. Happy attaches herself even physically to Emily; she "gurgled and chuckled and fastened herself around [Emily's] fingers," and Emily accepts that attachment and all that it implies about respect, affection, and commitment. In the end, Emily can only be happy with *both* the place and the people.

Caitlin Davies's novel *Jamestown Blues* is a circumspect and observant portrait of both the people and the place. Davies lived for eleven years in Botswana and has written a memoir about her experience (*Place of Reeds*, London: Simon & Schuster; Johannesburg and Cape Town: Jonathan Ball, 2005). *Jamestown Blues* (1995) was written while she still lived in Maun and is based to some extent on that experience. Her novel is told from the perspective of a young girl Dimpho (meaning "gifts," a common name in Setswana) whose mother is British and whose Motswana father works at a salt mine (probably Sowa Pan) as a manager; the Jamestown of the title probably refers to the northern town of Francistown, Botswana's second major city. Dimpho's life is fairly static—her father does not have much, if any, opportunity for advancement, since most of the other managers at the mine are white, and her mother is somewhat bored without any paid work. The conflict in the novel arises from the arrival of a white couple who befriend Dimpho's mother.

*Jamestown Blues* begins with the following lines: "God knows why, exactly, my mother decided to come to this country, but of course that was some time ago now and despite all that has happened in the past you could say she has settled down nicely" (3). This first sentence tells much about the novel and gives an interesting preview of the course of the story. The first three words express the kind of sentiment likely to be voiced by someone like Emily's mother, in *Dreams of the Kalahari*, who is so anxious to go Home. However, this sentence effectively switches the perspective from the place to the mother: "this country" is identified only in those terms, not as some God-forsaken hell. God's mysteries are associated thus with Rose, the mother, who eventually is able to "settle down nicely."

That phrase indicates how hard Davies works to locate the reader in *both* the physical and social environments of Botswana, describing the place both as it might seem to someone who lives here and as it probably looks to someone who only visits for a short time:

> Of course we in the tourist industry work hard to convince people that places like Lephane still *are* remote, because tourists like to think they are coming to a frontier, that they are being daring coming to a place where a lot of people go on living quite mundanely every day. The business section of Lephane has been carved up by the expatriates, which is a code word for white people most of the time, but where my grandmother lives it is crowded and still sandy. People like my grandmother are not exactly driving cars, so the sand doesn't bother them too much. However, these developments mean now they have to travel much further into the bush and the swamps in search of good palm wine and leaves to make baskets from and reeds to build with. (9–10)

In this paragraph, the contrasting pictures of Botswana are placed side by side, with a very sympathetic view of the problems that tourists bring to the social life of Batswana. Lephane is simultaneously a dangerous frontier and a boring, mundane town. The first sentence of this paragraph suggests the problems associated with the term "remote"; it poses the possibility that tourist companies have to create an image of Botswana that is not entirely true, one that creates difficulties for the people who are there.[7] That possibility comes to life in the literature

---

7. The narrator's explanation of how the tourist industry emphasises the

produced for overseas visitors, literature that shows the primitive Bushmen hunting with their bows and arrows.

The remainder of the first twenty-five pages or so are full of the kind of detail noted by a careful observer: turns of phrase (called "Tswinglish"), the layout of villages, the relationship of people to their governments, the experiences described by people who have studied abroad, the desire of parents to see their daughters become mothers, even if they cannot be persuaded to get married. In *Jamestown Blues*, every place is interesting because of the people who live there, and every place has a story to tell about the people who live on the land: "Although presumably people had always known there was salt on the pans, the government had only just decided to make a business of it. So first they had to get rid of the people who stayed around there, people whose land this had once been" (29). These are the same pans that, twenty years earlier, K. R. Butler in *A Desert of Salt* described and fictionalized as empty and desolate (see next chapter on adventure novels), but Davies writes people into the situation as if they were an afterthought to the building of the salt mine, which, of course, in the bureaucratic process, they are. The use of "So first" makes that attitude very clear. Emily, in *Dreams of the Kalahari*, also sees the people as an afterthought, but eventually that afterthought becomes the precondition to her own happiness.

Davies continually weaves into her story observations about how the narrator's Motswana father does things and how the narrator understands and observes people responding to her parents. The novel presents a range of lifestyles and beliefs, as in the following passages:

It was late November. There had hardly been any rain

---

exotic quality of the locale also recalls the way Africa is represented in film, most notably in popular documentaries (see introduction).

at all since that one evening and most everyone in the township was talking about the weather. Rib-thin donkeys wandered through the streets of Jamestown and looked as if they were about to keel over. On the radio the President advised people to pray.

Jamestown had a relatively reliable water supply, though, unlike the nearby villages whose boreholes seemed to be drying up. Ignoring the authorities' appeal to use less water, the expatriates continued to clean their cars at weekends and sprinkle their lush green lawns. Jamestown was a haven of luxury in a desert. The expatriates knew little of the empty hands, the dying cattle and the hungry people. (138)

Then an elephant turned up a few kilometres from the salt mine, flapping its ears and looking for water. Some of the Boers, who were very righteous when it came to wild animals, urged the mine to herd the elephant to water.

My mother was very excited by the news. "Just imagine, an elephant!" she said and sat down to write a letter to her mother.

"It's not so unusual," my father said dismissively, though I was also excited and longing to go and see it. "This used to be their ranges after all." (139)

The attitudes expressed in this passage show, again, the contrast between how different groups of people coexist—or do not coexist—in Botswana. The Boers[8] behave as they imagine concerned environmentalists would behave; Dimpho's mother is still English enough to be interested and to write a letter home about it—reinforcing foreign views about what Botswana must be like—nevertheless, she does not go to see it. Dimpho's father is much more pragmatic about the elephant's ability to take care of itself. Dimpho herself, of course, like any child, would

---

8. The term "Boers" in contemporary Botswana usage is often, though

like to go see it. This passage typifies how Davies writes about the interactions between whites and blacks in Botswana: she takes as her starting point the Batswana (the narrator's father is, after all, Motswana), and therefore they must be present in the novel.[9]

*Okavango Gods* by Anthony Fleischer was published only two years after *Jamestown Blues*, but the atmosphere of *Okavango Gods* is quite different. Fleischer is a South African writer who is possibly best known for his novel *Children of Adamastor*. He has also worked in mining to restructure that industry's labor organization. In *Okavango Gods*, he moves into the world of the Hambukushu of the Okavango Delta, in northwest Botswana, and has attempted to write sympathetically about and from this minority community in Botswana.[10] The novel is set in the period just after the release of Nelson Mandela, when South African exiles in Botswana refugee camps were preparing to return home. Pula Barotse is set to become the next rainmaker, after his father passes on, and he is friends with Julia Pinto, daughter of

---

not always, a derogatory term and refers to white people whose mother tongue is Afrikaans. It originally meant peasant farmers of Dutch ancestry. Boer mythology about themselves contains a significant component of being stewards of the land (including its animals), so the behavior here is doubly ironic.

9. Attitudes to wildlife can also be categorized according to a north-south division within the country. People from the south are increasingly vacationing in the north of the country to see the big game, since most of that game lives in the north; in the north, however, that wildlife is frequently seen as a problem because of the damage caused to crops, livestock, and so forth, and therefore it is not so exotic. The north-south division also points to a class division, with wealthier urban residents paying for safari vacations, and small farmers coping with problem wildlife in order to survive.

10. Thomas J. Larson, an anthropologist, has also written a novel for children, *Dibebe of the Okavango*, which chronicles the journey of a young Mbukushu herd boy, Dibebe, as he travels through the Okavango Delta from Shakawe to Maun to train as a traditional healer.

a Portuguese doctor. Pula and Julia are trapped when the region around Shakawe is flooded. Fleischer weaves together themes of the power of the rainmaker among the Hambukushu, of the Biblical flood (cleansing), the life of Gilgamesh, and the conflict of modern ways with traditional (Hambukushu) beliefs. He is clearly fascinated by what he perceives as the power of Hambukushu rainmakers[11] and other traditional figures: the diviner Bubi (a woman, unusually) is a frightening figure who anoints Julia as the next *mugrodi*; according to the novel, a *mugrodi* is a wife of the rainmaker whose children must be sacrificed for rainmaking.[12]

In many ways, this novel is a fantasy. The mythical and real worlds—the traditional and the modern—collide in the relationships that are explored: Pula and Julia, Bubi and Julia, John (Pula's father) and Sergio (Julia's father), Julia and Potlako Lereeng (a refugee who is said to have "Basotho magic," the most powerful of all), Bubi and Potlako, and Julia and the pilot of the rescue plane. The novel shows a great deal of respect for the power of belief, and belief here is an aspect of life on the water, the life that the Hambukushu live. In southern Africa, water brings life, but in *Okavango Gods*, the waters bring death. The opportunity to renew life is overshadowed by the incredible destruction that the floods leave in their aftermath.

Once again, however, Botswana, in particular the Okavango Delta, is a place that must be overcome. In order for life to continue, it must overcome the flood, the desert of water. Even without the floods, though, the river and the delta are places of danger: Lereeng and his gang rustle Tswana cattle there, and of course there are the familiar dangers in the crocodiles that lie in

---

11. There is a historical basis for this perception: in the nineteenth century, Hambukushu rainmakers used their power for political leverage in Angola.

12. See Larson, *Hambukushu Rainmakers of the Okavango*.

wait on the banks of the river and in the hippos that lurk under the surface of the water.

And again, in the opening lines of the novel, death is omnipresent: Pula is in his *mokoro* (canoe) watching two praying mantises mate on a pile of papyrus reeds in the bottom of the boat. The moment of rapture is, as Pula well knows, overshadowed by the imminent death of the male, who will be devoured by the female: his "triumph would not last long" (3). Indeed, nothing of the life that Pula knows will last long; the death of the male praying mantis foreshadows a number of other deaths that will occur as a result of the flood that is bearing down on Shakawe from Angola. Pula's father has made rain, but it will be too much of a good thing.

The specter of death hangs over the whole novel, in fact. The mood of the novel does not evoke joy, not joy for Pula's and Julia's growing affection, not joy for the coming of the rain—which is destructive in any case—not joy for Pula's ascension to the position of rainmaker. The overwhelming feeling that the novel evokes is one of sadness and loss: at one point, Pula wants to prevent Julia from leaving, and he tries to grab her arm: "His thumb and forefinger, which had held a tiny but precious piece of the cloth of her sleeve, stayed pinched in the air, forlorn, hesitant," and when Julia looks back at him, she sees him "as if he were grasping for something just lost. He looked so pathetic, so African, so wild" (22).

Rather than celebrating what is possible in the relationship between Pula and Julia, therefore, the novel focuses on something that is incomplete and even pathetic. Bubi believes that the old rituals for making rain must be reinstated (Pula is the last child of the last *mugrodi*[13]). When she sees the affection

---

13. There is an irony here: Pula, as a child of the *mugrodi*, should not have survived infancy.

developing between Pula and Julia, she anoints Julia, a white woman who does not believe in the powers of rainmaking, as the next *mugrodi*, as Pula's wife. Julia is apparently the only person who can save Hambukushu society; even Pula recognizes that if he cannot catch and hold her, he will lose something valuable. Africa—Botswana, the Hambukushu—cannot survive without Julia's help. In the terms of her own world, she becomes a saint, sent to save Africa from itself. The pilot of the rescue plane observes this aspect of her and comments on it when Julia, suffering from sleeping sickness, asks him to find her doctor father:

> This was no girl lost in the swamp, this was a woman of purpose struck down by some terrible African disease. I could do nothing and I could say nothing. I was struck dumb, if you like, again struck by the beauty of her, the touch of death perhaps, or by the faint and all-forgiving smile of eternal womanhood. Here, this saintly presence, this yearned-for virgin in white, this unexpected gentleness, in my aeroplane! (104)

Julia is the focus of all attention, both white and Hambukushu. She is all that is good—gentle—but suffering all the problems of Africa—a terrible disease. She is the saintly picture of eternal womanhood, but contrasted with her future as a *mugrodi*, a woman who kills her own children.

Ironically, Julia's father is unable to help her. Only Bubi, using traditional medicines, brings Julia back from the brink of death. The "terrible African disease" can only be cured by a "terrible" African, but yet we are asked to believe that Africa can only be saved by a fifteen-year-old white girl. Julia's intractable resistance to the suggestions that Bubi makes to her and to the things that Bubi must do to prepare her for her new life again evoke no anticipation, only sadness about the inevitability of the death that will follow her (all the newborn children of a *mugrodi* are brutally sacrificed in order to ensure rain) and sadness about the state that Hambukushu society (and Africa in general) seems to have fallen into. Fleischer's solution to these problems seems to suggest a nonracial future, but whether such a future can be realized if Julia does not accept or even believe—is, in fact, afraid of—what she is supposed to do appears unlikely.

Curiously, Fleischer here echoes Sello, in Bessie Head's *A Question of Power*, where Sello tries to make Elizabeth see what love is ("two people mutually feeding each other" [197]). Sello, like Bubi, is a figure of both good and evil aspects, one whom Elizabeth ultimately comes to love and respect, much the same way that Pula respects and fears Bubi. What makes the end of *Okavango Gods* more problematic, however, is not Pula's ambivalence towards Bubi, but Julia's reluctance to take on the mantle that Bubi is preparing for her. Head's Elizabeth eventually becomes the prophet for the brotherhood of man, but Julia is preparing to refuse, thus endangering all of Bubi's plans. The happy ending planned in the marriage of Pula and Julia comes at great cost to Julia—and thus also to Pula and the Hambukushu.[14]

Abena Busia writes of adventure novels of the mid-twentieth century that they show a continent in which morality is absent and must be put in place by the West. In *Okavango Gods*, Fleisher gives us the character of Pula, whose own existence represents a triumph of Western morality over ritual. How Pula is capable of becoming a rainmaker when his very life demonstrates a powerful challenge to rainmaking rituals is a contradiction that Fleischer does not examine, but rather he seems to reinforce the notion of a "moral victory" by creating a white

---

14. The question of whether *Okavango Gods* ends positively can include a comparison to the end of Head's *Maru* as well, when Margaret saves her people at a horrible cost to her own happiness.

woman, one who ironically does not accept the responsibility of becoming the next *mugrodi*.

William Duggan has attempted to write a similar mytho-poetic saga of the people of southern Africa; his novels *The Great Thirst* and *Lovers of the African Night* are written almost entirely from the perspective of the fictional BaNare (people of the buffalo). Duggan is familiar with the history of southern Africa, and he has conceived of this story in a way that combines Setswana traditional epics with the vision of a writer like James A. Michener. In a brief notice in the *New York Times Book Review*, Mark Bowen writes that Duggan "adopts the techniques and assumes the voice of an old African storyteller sitting before a campfire" (30), and he describes the BaNare's view of their past, which is based on the history of southern Africa to the end of World War II, as "one inexorable catastrophe after the next" (30). How does one respond to such a characterization of African life?

*The Great Thirst* and *Lovers of the African Night* are the first two novels of a proposed trilogy (the third has not yet appeared), and they give the history of a family in what is now Botswana from the mid-nineteenth century to the mid-1970s and the fight against apartheid in South Africa. *The Great Thirst* begins with a young Motswana boy named Mojamaje of the BaNare, who will become the chief of his clan the Tladis and the father of many generations. The novel covers his coming of age, his marriage, and the fortunes of his children. It gives an overview of society at the time: traders, migrants, and such come into and go out of the lives of the BaNare, but Duggan's attempt to bring southern African history to life is not entirely successful.

One reason for this lack of success is revealed most clearly in *Lovers of the African Night*, in which the events of post–World War II South Africa are used to show the realities of political change in terms of ordinary lives. Sheila Solomon Klass, in her review for the *New York Times Book Review*, writes that "Historic events such as the Sharpeville massacre and the Soweto student protest—as the BaNare participate in them firsthand—become part of the common African experience and are thus transmuted into myth; the martyred miraculously live on" (11). Unfortunately, as these historic events are retold, they become trivial. In the fictional world, Ata Four[15] starts the Sharpeville massacre by being the first to set fire to her pass and then leaving the scene, thus devaluing the gestures of all the people who really did set fire to their passes and stayed and were shot, and her son Kanye becomes Hector Petersen, only Kanye survives, glossing over and diminishing the impact of Petersen's very real murder. Possibly this technique is an attempt to give individuality and context to abstract history, but again, since Hector Petersen already had a name and an individuality, Kanye's centrality to the events is at best superfluous. Usually in historical fiction, either characters are minor and their presence would not have been recorded, so that a writer may take more artistic license, or else the characters are major and they do exactly what was recorded as happening. The insertion of characters into major historical events that we see in *Lovers of the African Night* is reminiscent of *Forrest Gump*, in which footage of Tom Hanks as Forrest Gump is pasted into actual historical footage, to comic effect.

By displacing the events of the real past and of real people onto fictional characters, Duggan's story loses much of its impact. The novels become uneasy, awkward marriages of family saga, oral epic, and historical novel, without the characteristics of any that make them engrossing reads.

Norman Rush is a novelist who worked for four years in Botswana, as director of the Peace Corps office, and his first

---

15. Duggan's names are generally somewhat odd: Batswana do not usually name their children sequentially, and some of the names in *The Great Thirst* are curious, possibly mnemonic—Hrikwa the Griqua, Tsolo the Zulu, and so forth.

published work, the stories *Whites* of 1986, describes, through various viewpoints, white expatriate life in a Botswana that had been independent for nearly twenty years. Rush's stories, and his two novels *Mating* and *Mortals*, rely very heavily on the familiar structure of "Africa" as a place where whites go to understand and even discover themselves;[16] the Batswana themselves are relevant only to the extent that they assist or hinder the search for expatriate identity. For Slaughter, Fleischer, and Rush, the hellish countryside must be overcome in the test of self, but in Rush the desert triggers a crisis of identity in the white expatriate, and the identities of the Batswana become indistinguishable from that landscape. In *Mating*, the desert is a barrier between the narrator and Tsau, an artificial community run by women where the elusive Nelson Denoon can be found. In general, Rush grapples with a problem that probably confronts many people who go to work in Botswana: Where can we and do we fit in? In *Mating* and in the short story "Near Pala," he uses two different narrator figures to observe and comment on Tswana life—both white women, one an anthropologist who has studied the Batswana and thus has become sort of an "expert,"[17] and the other the wife of a contractor who wants to help some women who are begging for water. His preoccupation remains the whites, and as a study of them, his works are very interesting and funny, and perhaps even cut a bit too close for comfort. But the impression remains very strongly that the narrators, although curious, are not really concerned about

---

16. This model is familiar in Western literature: many people have the experience of redefining themselves in a new place; see, for example, *French Lessons*, by Alice Kaplan, for an example of a contemporary, nonfictional exploration of this phenomenon. And, of course, the experience is also familiar because it is based on a common real experience.

17. I am well aware of my own role here as narrator of Botswana literature.

where they are, a fact which makes one wonder whether they even like it. It is easy enough to say that in a novel about expatriates, he is entitled to write about them, but unfortunately, in Botswana, in Africa, it is not so simple because of the history of unequal relationships between whites and blacks. John Leonard, in his review of *Mortals*, writes that the novel presents "a southern Africa on which as if it were a sand screen, the West projects its own dementias" (paragraph 1). "Finding oneself" in Europe or America does not come with the baggage of imperial and neo-imperial history that is necessarily attached to relationships with Africa. Too often, as in the first part of *Dreams of the Kalahari*, Africans have simply been ignored in their own homes. In Rush's works, as in so many others, the place must again be conquered if one is to understand one's own self. The other people who live there do not really matter and can continue to be ignored in their own homes.

Although the story "Near Pala" is not a novel, the imagery that Rush uses to place white expatriates in the context of Botswana is vivid and useful for understanding the problems of writing about whites in Africa—in Botswana in particular. The first sentences of "Near Pala" concern four whites returning from a trip to the bush: "Here the road was a soft red trough. In a Land-Rover laboring along it were four whites, the men in front, the women in back" (17). The trough is resistant, hence the vehicle is "laboring," and they must keep moving in order not to get stuck in the sand. The narrative perspective belongs to Nan, the wife of the driver. She is interested in where she lives, and she describes it as follows:

> "Coming back here to Botswana from holiday, it was so strange and nice. We were in the plane, coming low over the land. I was happy to see Botswana again. It was so strange, Tess—the country seemed like a poor relation, someone nice who refuses gifts at first, someone you like. This country is so poor. We were flying low over it. And

then all I could think of was our friend the peerless Dr. Hartogs, who said that from the air the country looks as if it has ringworm." (19)[18]

Nan's description is both affectionate ("nice," "happy," "like") and patronizing ("poor relation…who refuses gifts"). She notices the contrast with the description of her doctor friend,[19] who describes the physical appearance of a *lolwapa*, a homestead, as a fungus, an unwanted growth on the otherwise clean and healthy land. Her affection for the place, though, is obviously preferable to the other perspective, represented by Tom, the other man in the Land Rover: "Tom said, '*We* put in the roads and *they* don't maintain them, do *they*? *They* think a road is a thing like your fingernail—chip it and it grows back. Well, *they*'re wrong, aren't *they*?'" (19, emphasis added). Tom uses the words "we" and "they" in a way that is familiar from conventional stereotypes: the dividing line between the good group and the bad group is made clear. He is easily recognizable as the bad white, the racist expat, etc., and he is contrasted with Nan. This dichotomy is emphasized again at various points throughout the story:

> "Look at the courtyards, Tess. They are as neat as you like. They sweep them morning and evening."
>
> "Yes, everything goes into the lane," Gareth said. (20)

> "When we first moved in at the mine, we did something at the house so stupid I am still in pain. There were two pawpaw trees growing side by side by the house, one thriving

---

18. The skepticism about the viability of independent African states finds more overt expression in *Dreams of the Kalahari*, when Emily's lover asks her if she really wants to follow him from London back to southern Africa: "'And it's a black state, too, remember,'" he cautions her (223).

19. The name of the doctor is also, significantly, an Afrikaner name, which reminds readers of the unpleasant characteristics associated with Afrikaners.

with nice big pawpaws on it and the other sick-looking and leaf-less—dead-looking. Well, we thought it was plain what we should do: take down the dead tree. So we...uprooted it, Gareth and myself....We didn't understand. It seems the pawpaw grow in pairs, couples, male and female. The male tree looks like a phallus—no foliage to it, really. The female needs the male in order to bear. They take years to reach the height ours had. Then the female died. The staff had been eating pawpaws from our tree for years. It was a humiliation."

"Bit ancient times by now, isn't it?" Gareth said angrily. (21)

This incident can be read as a parable about the problem of aid workers in Africa, who arrive with all sorts of preconceived ideas, and risk destroying other important and valuable ideas. The tone of contrast created by the ongoing argument between Nan and the men sets up Nan as the outsider even within her own social circle—she probably also gets on everybody's nerves—and the definition of her character depends on her difference from them in terms of her attitude toward where she is and toward the other people who live there. She also shows concern for her fellow travelers by, for example, refusing to drink water, in spite of her pregnancy (24), because she understands the importance of not stopping in the deep sand (so that she may urinate), but her consideration is ridiculed by those to whom she otherwise "belongs." The core of the story comes when they are moving along a particularly treacherous stretch of the track, and they see some figures waving to them in the distance:

"It's *bushies!*" Tom said.

"No, it's too far south—can't be," Gareth said.

"No, it is, it is—it's bushies," Tom said. "They must be clear over from the pan. It must be the drought. I hear the pan is dried up. God, that is a distance to come. Dear

God above. It is. There's a string of them. Want us to stop." (27)

The women were close to the road. Two of them were holding out pots or cans. The girls were waving the vessels up and down, stiffly, frantically. The mother dropped into an odd posture, like kneeling prayer, but clapping her hands under chin. They made a tableau. The Rover approached. The women were dressed in skins and rags. They were thin. Nan stared. Arms and legs were like sticks. Their hair seemed to grow in dots on their skulls. One girl appeared to be wearing a kind of cap, but it was a huge scab, Nan saw. All were smiling unnaturally at the vehicle as it passed slowly. They were calling out. Nan opened her window. It was impossible to understand anything. (28)

Tess is sorry that they cannot stop, since she assumes that they want to trade. In fact they want water (*metse*, which Tess thinks she does not have), and Nan begs Gareth to stop, but he refuses. The ironic tone of the story that is created by the use of those familiar stereotypes of white expatriates make the readers shake their heads at Tom, Gareth, and Tess, but the use of the word "tableau" calls the perspective of the narrative voice into question, recalling the screen on which the West inscribes itself (Leonard). In this horrible situation, the San become like animals on the land[20]: they form a scene, the sort of thing one sees on safari, or pictured in tourist literature; they are suffering from the drought, like the dead cattle that the party has

---

20. The attitude expressed in this passage is still common today among both expatriates and Batswana. Controversies about "what to do" about the San continue to rage concerning whether they should be allowed to remain in the Central Kalahari Game Reserve, whether they ought to be brought up to the same level of development that the rest of the people of Botswana enjoy, and so forth.

seen on the journey; they are far out of their "normal range," the pans.[21] The event can just become another anecdote from "wild" Botswana: Tess says, "pity we can't stop"; she wants to trade. So these "bushies" will get no water, even though Nan throws them one of the bottles that is in the Rover, even though she is not drinking, and even though they are traveling with several jerrycans full of water. The story ends with Gareth after all bringing the Rover to a halt in the sand trough: the story suggests that Nan will have to get out of the vehicle and fetch the water bottle again, despite Gareth's insistence that they cannot stop to help. The description of the incident undercuts the tone of irony; in the end, the picture is just like so many others that people see when they look toward Africa: a poor, starving, drought-ridden nightmare.

*Mating* (1991) is Rush's second work about Botswana and his first novel (it won the 1991 National Book Award in the United States), and in it the place becomes even more of a backdrop for a white character's experiences. In this novel, the female narrator meets a man who runs a development project in a remote location, and she wants to be a part of it. The novel chronicles her journey to the place and her relationship with the man, Nelson Denoon. Rush drew inspiration for his fictional community from real attempts to introduce new ways of development, most specifically, the projects in Swaneng (in Serowe) run by Patrick van Rensburg in the 1960s,[22] although

---

21. Caitlin Davies's scene in her novel *Jamestown Blues* (when the elephant comes to the pan to drink) is similar.
22. For more information about the Brigades Movement, see Bessie Head, *Serowe: Village of the Rain Wind,* and *Sheila Bagnall's Letters from Botswana, 1966–1974.* Patrick van Rensburg continues to work in education and development and writes about it for local papers. See also van Rensburg's own publications and his more recent work for the Foundation for Education with Production.

the fictional project is far more radical.

*Mating* begins as follows: "In Africa you want more, I think" (5). This desire for knowledge—an almost insatiable desire that is prefigured in the more gentle curiosity of Nan in "Near Pala"—drives the book, and also gives it a rather arrogant tone; Agbaw and Kiesinger, in an article comparing *Mating* to *Heart of Darkness*, write that this opening portrays Africa "as a place where white people lose the inhibitions and restraints of civilization to indulge in all kinds of excesses" (3): in the case of *Mating*, though, it seems the whites indulge in all sorts of intellectual games; Tsau is, after all, a radical experiment in development, in social engineering, even if set in the middle of the treacherous desert. Africa, Botswana, becomes merely a place to be mined for gold, diamonds, adventure, information, a place also where whites learn about themselves. The narrator decides early on that she is going to "be a docent, presenting Botswana as an institution with obscure holdings" (10). She needs to create a role for herself to validate her life in Gaborone, since her research seems to be falling apart, and she deliberately decides to use her knowledge to refashion Botswana society into something odd that will also be interesting to outsiders.

The critic Trinh Minh-ha discusses the situation of "the Other" who must represent an entire society to tourists seeking something different:

> Eager not to disappoint, i [sic] try my best to offer my benefactors and benefactresses what they most anxiously yearn for: the possibility of difference, yet a difference or an otherness that will not go so far as to question the foundation of their beings and makings. Their situation is not unlike that of the American tourists who, looking for a change of scenery and pace in a foreign land, such as, for example, Japan, strike out in search of what they believe to be the "real" Japan—most likely shaped after

the vision of Japan as handed to them and reflected in television films like "Shogun"—or that of the anthropologists....Authenticity in such contexts turns out to be a product that one can buy, arrange to one's liking, and/or preserve. (267)

In *Mating*, the narrator, although not Motswana, thinks that she can be particularly useful to expatriates because she knows so much: "I had the specific wherewithal for this. I spoke good Setswana. I had anecdotes. I could demonstrate that beneath the surface the culture was as other as anyone could ask" (11). She expresses her own conviction that she knows everything about the society, and she also insists on its difference, so Batswana become irrelevant to her agenda. She begins her new vocation by pointing out a group of people who can be identified by their uniforms; they are members of the Zion Christian Church (ZCC), a major regional church:

> Fifty marchers went slowly by. Men in taut tan porters' uniforms and garrison caps led. Women followed, all in white. The women wore ordinary sandals. I pointed out the footgear of the men....I also explained that once they started singing they sang without pause for as long as a couple of hours. My group said things like Where do they get the energy? The marchers were through leaping for the day. But I told my group where they could catch them some other Sunday. I knew what routes they took. (12)

In this passage, the narrator is a new kind of a tour guide. She points out the churches the way a safari guide might point out a likely watering spot for lions and elephants. The ZCC members also form a picture or a video very like the tableau created by the begging women in "Near Pala." The narrator's activities are reminiscent of those in cultural tourism, but she is not a member of a community giving visitors a view into her own world; rather, she is presenting and explaining a foreign society to the outside world as if it were an artifact, rather than a living human community—ultimately making it even more foreign. Dimpho, in *Jamestown Blues*, exposes the process clearly when she describes the tour operator's recognition (in her case, also the resident's view) of what a remote village must appear to be if it is going to be interesting at all.

Eventually, the narrator decides that she must go off in search of Denoon and his Tsau project; her search involves crossing the Kalahari. This Botswana is rather more like a nightmare, as it is in adventure novels, including of course *Heart of Darkness*. Admittedly, this narrator is trying to make her way alone in the middle of a dangerous environment, but she arrogantly assumes she knows everything and forgets all the rules of survival. Her arrogance about what she knows about Botswana reveals in this particular passage a dislike for where she is. If something looks odd, there must be something wrong with it; perhaps the people are diseased:

> In the outskirts of Kang something happened that I took as a reminder not to interpret experiential oddities too quickly. I was approaching the path leading to the primary school, and I stopped to watch the children running to class, a stream of them, and I thought Oh god! No! because as they passed I was seeing a stream of little hunchbacks, every one of them hunchbacked. I thought So many hunchbacks in one little spot in the Kalahari. What a commentary! Why was this never reported? How can this be? But then I watched as one little girl's hump disappeared. A tin bowl appeared at her feet and one of her schoolmates kicked it in my direction. In Kang it was the custom to carry your mealie bowl to school on your back with your jersey pulled tight over it to hold it in place, that was all. So with that I set off into the unknown, telling myself to remember that there is less to the mysterious than meets the eye. (132–33)

The narrator's description of the incident shows very good skills of observation ("How can this be?" is a phrase commonly used by Batswana speakers of English) as well as an understanding of what can be wrong with perceptions in a foreign environment. And yet she does not ask; she does not follow her own advice. Seeing a group of schoolchildren who look odd immediately brings her to the conclusion that something must be wrong with them. Botswana is a land infected— with hunchbacks, with ringworm—she expects to see disease rather than lunch tins or homesteads. Furthermore, she contradicts herself in her self-assigned role as docent, since she has already commented that because Botswana is not as different as foreigners would like, she must create that difference and point it out. Obviously she is quite successful.

The narrator's trek through the desert is an attempt, in some ways, to conquer the landscape, but it is also a process of identity definition—she must survive the Kalahari, not conquer it, because she wants to conquer Denoon for herself. The emptiness and heat of the bush and desert recall very clearly the inferno that a number of adventure writers describe. There are, in addition to the deadly heat, lions and vultures waiting to devour her and her two donkeys; she almost does not make it to Tsau. Botswana here must be endured in order to win the prize that the narrator wants. The desire for knowledge is mostly desire for self-knowledge, not knowledge about where she lives, about which she claims to be an expert, and about which she therefore does not need to learn more, and which she turns into a rather unpleasant museum.

Denoon, the prize, lives in a community he has created. He is also an outsider expert and, not unlike the narrator, tries to present a foreign community as something of his own design. Tsau, his creation, exists in the middle of the desert, isolated almost completely from any other community. It is also a community of women, over which he benignly—almost passively—

reigns as RraPuleng.[23] He has organized the community along lines that he believes are best. The narrator identifies the nature of the place:

> Tsau was no self-help settlement, not with slab concrete floors as level as ponds in every rondavel. This was not a perfect yet cheap idea working itself out. This was enlightened surplus capital coming in to lift a whole subclass of people up onto a pedestal and saying Go. What I was thinking over and over was This is all very well—but. Tsau was a charity, or a species of it, which Denoon had to turn into something generically different or it was hardly worth doing. (196)

The narrator's astute observation skills serve her well here. The project is essentially Denoon's. He needs to make it into something in order for his own ideas to be validated. He has obviously poured a great deal of money into making it work (whose money is not quite clear), and the narrator's observations raise provocative issues about the nature and success of "aid" in the classic sense; her observations also recall the story of the pawpaw trees, where a healthy pawpaw tree is cut down because no one thought to ask what was going on. The failure of the enterprise would reflect Denoon's own failure to face other tensions and processes at work in the society—at work in any society—that are completely beyond his control, such as, for example, tensions between men and women (in any event, one wonders how a society without men can survive). The narrator seems both to admire him for the nobility of his ideas and to want to force him to face his lack of understanding, in a bid, perhaps,

---

23. The name RraPuleng means "father of the place of rain" and was the name given to a well-known Peace Corps volunteer in the late 1960s, who is not the model for Nelson Denoon.

to force him to be honest with her in the way that she demands but does not reciprocate.

As the relationship between Denoon and the narrator develops, it begins to incorporate a complex set of intellectual games that are played out on the stage of Tsau. The function in their relationship of Tsau and the women who live there becomes particularly clear when a population of monkeys moves in and starts to cause problems. Some of the women raise the question of whether guns should be available for shooting the monkeys. They speak to the narrator; she then raises their concerns and suggestions with Denoon, who rejects the idea:

> Guns are not a good idea, he said, very curt. Then it was Who, exactly, talked to you?
>
> Reason with me and I might tell you, I said.
>
> He didn't want to. He wanted me to accept the general proposition. I was firm. (255)

> Then I said , which I should not have, People say you have a rifle yourself.
>
> Who told you that? he said, apparently outraged. I hated his murderous expression with its inner taint of shame....
>
> Well, was it true he had a gun, or not? In fact it was. He hardly even knew why. The construction crew had left it with him, all right sold it to him, rather. It was for some emergency purpose. It was just an ultimate precaution. It was like having a fire extinguisher. And he wanted to know, seriously, whom I had heard it from.
>
> I evaded that and asked him why in the name of god he didn't just take the thing and appease people by shooting a few vervets. I said Your deus ex machina is sitting on a shelf somewhere and you won't use it. (256–57)

In this passage, the narrator insists that their discussion of the issue must be logical ("Reason with me"), and Denoon reveals only bit by bit how he acquired the gun and how he feels about it.[24] Denoon's evasiveness contrasts sharply with the narrator's own more subtle evasiveness about what she will tell him. His possessing the gun does not seem logical, given his expressed feelings about hunting and killing. But the fact that he has it and wants to know who knows that he has it points to the role he sees for himself in the community. He is still the benevolent protector, living a kind of polygynous relationship with the women of Tsau, especially the "Mother Committee," the good king who can, if necessary, reassert his control by using his *deus ex machina* to set things back to order on the stage of the community. The discussion between the narrator and Denoon points to their own irrelevance: Denoon's because the narrator ignores his suggestion about poison in favor of supporting the women's request for a gun, and the narrator's because of her evasion and attempts to use Tsau to "conquer" Denoon.

The nature of gender relations in *Mating* is also curious. Tsau is a matriarchal society—except that Denoon himself sits above the hierarchy. Men are not allowed into the community except in so far as they have a specific job to do, and they are not given any positions of responsibility with respect to the community. Within the community, this situation is undoubtedly an attempt to reverse the biases that work within Botswana society, but the matriarchy refers also to other "real-life" problems: for example, it has been difficult to get aid funding for projects that do not improve the status of women, regardless of how useful and important other projects might be. In such instances, it seems to be a case of the West imposing its own values onto a society, and certainly Denoon's artificial community

---

24. He also seems surprised that the women know he has it. His experience of small-town or village life is obviously rather limited, since in such an environment, everyone knows everything about everyone else. Probably everyone in Botswana knows he has a gun.

is an example of that: the narrator writes that Tsau is essentially propped up by capital that Denoon raised himself so that he could apply his ideas and *make* them work.

If the narrator turns Botswana into an unpleasant museum, Denoon similarly turns Tsau into a different kind of morality play, in which the characters are allowed to make mistakes and then see the error of their ways while he, the director and deity, dictates for and corrects them. Denoon's ideas are played out on the (artificial) stage of Tsau, a stage which he can protect with his *deus ex machina*. The gun's existence occasions the conflict between Denoon and his pursuer and foreshadows the end of the novel, when the narrator returns to Denoon: "Nelson knows that you lie to me at your peril. I will not have it" (477). Rush's Botswana is a stage set that can be created and re-created to suit the needs of the players, and Denoon is any foreign aid organization that can create and re-create a country according to the dictates of development theory fashion. Once again, the place and its people do not really matter.

In his most recent novel *Mortals* (2003), Botswana recedes even further to become a place almost like the setting of the modern techno-thriller. As a place, it has less importance for the midlife crisis of the narrator, a teacher and United States undercover agent who is supposed to be gathering information about antigovernment activity. The narrator is an American living abroad, and the relationships that he has with his wife and with his family back in the United States begin to crumble while he is investigating a particular man. Botswana provides the impetus for a number of crises involving imagined revolutionary groups (reminding the reader of Steve White's *The Battle in Botswana* and Jeff Rovin's *Mission of Honor*).[25] In the

---

25. In a review of *Mortals* for the *New York Times*, Michiko Kakutani writes that "Ray's plotting...will provoke an insurrection and result in

end, *Mortals* is a more thorough exploration of the response of one individual to changes in his once-secure life, and Leonard's assessment, that Africa is presented as a canvas on which the West (in this case, middle-aged male America) writes its own dementias, does not account for the fact that Ray's crisis could have happened anywhere—including America—because the Botswana where Ray's life falls apart does not really exist. Why then does it happen in Botswana?

Rush is not the first person to set a novel of midlife crisis in a foreign country. Many people do experience profound changes when they go abroad. In *Mortals*, Botswana itself becomes a place of conflict, with revolutionary groups operating in the north, in order to precipitate and in some ways precipitated by the personal crisis and conflict of his character. If the conflict is because of the latter scenario, then Botswana does become just a screen for Ray's own dementia. If the conflict is necessary for the former case, it is important to consider the problem of taking such artistic license in the context of already-problematic relationships between the "first" world and the "third." In either case, the place is utterly irrelevant.

A final, very short, novel was written by Alfred M. Merriweather, a medical missionary who founded a hospital at Molepolole and was well known nationally both as a personal friend of Seretse Khama and as Speaker of Parliament. *Desert Harvest* (1977) describes the life of a family through each of its members: each chapter is devoted to the life of one of the family members (composites of real people Merriweather knew). This book has very little plot and is more descriptive of the life that people live. Merriweather pays very close attention to the people around him. He reports about what he has observed and

---

the deaths of many innocents. None of this is portrayed in remotely believable terms..." (paragraph 9).

sets it in the context of what he is familiar with from his interactions with the people around him and with whom he works. In this way, his own perspective fades into the background so that the life around him can become the focus of the book. Merriweather became a citizen, spoke Setswana, and involved himself in the spiritual, political, and health affairs of his community during the many years that he lived here. His perspective of Botswana, developed through observing the life of the people he knew, offers a very brief but very refreshing contrast to the more self-absorbed approach of much other fiction of Botswana.

What is written about Botswana by people with apparently limited experience of the place, without their own acknowledgement of their limitations, strikes me as dishonest.[26] The lopsided nature of the Africa–West relationship makes an awareness and disclosure of one's own perspective crucial. Fiction by its nature offers infinite freedom for exploring the attitudes of made-up people about a place that a writer can re-create to suit the needs of the story, but an interrogation of the fantasies, prejudices, and preconceptions that inform writing is just as important as the freedom to write. We learn about other places from fiction. We need to be aware of what we learn.

---

26. This chapter has been the most difficult to write, given my own very problematic relationship to Botswana and the fact that I am probably more like the characters in these books than I would like to admit. My own reaction to what outsiders write about Botswana is strongly shaped by how I feel about the place and the ignorance—or compassion—that I perceive a writer to display. To ignore my own strong emotions about a place where I have lived for more than ten years is equally dishonest, and I do not wish to feign any sort of objectivity about what I think.

# PAPER SAFARI—ADVENTURE NOVELS
## OF BOTSWANA

Adventure literature set in southern Africa is a genre that can trace its roots back to the hunting literature of the nineteenth century. Southern Africa has proved a fertile ground for testing the mettle of (usually) young men who set off in search of something more out-of-the-ordinary. Jules Verne's novel *Meridiana* is a science adventure, and the events, setting, and opinions contained within it place it quite squarely within the tradition of exploration and safari writing that began for southern Africa in the middle of the nineteenth century. In Verne's novel, three Englishmen and three Russians have arrived in southern Africa in order to determine the arc of a meridian in the Kalahari Desert; they are accompanied by a "Bushman" guide. When war breaks out between England and Russia, each group races to be the first to complete the job. The exotic nature of the people and problems that they encounter establishes the parameters for much of the adventure literature about Botswana that followed in the twentieth century.

Dan Wylie, in his examination of the iconography of the elephant in South African eco-literature, identifies hunters as "pioneers who inaugurated that patronage" (86) of European imperial activity in Africa, a point made also by Stephen Gray in chapter 5 of his study *Southern African Literature: an Introduction*. For Gray, hunting literature is directly in the service of imperialism, for which it forges a path (107) and which glorifies the role of fair play, epitomized by the hunter's mercy toward and respect for the animals that he hunts—not, of course, toward his "native" guide, who himself, however, develops respect for the hunter's bravery and whose respect translates into a form of subservience in the imperial relationship between "native" and white.

The legacy of this relationship can clearly be seen in more contemporary adventure literature. Abena Busia phrases it in more psychological terms: the "trauma" (danger, wildness, etc.) of Africa leads to the psychically whole white (168). This myth, she argues, has changed little over the course of the past century or more, and is the basis for the modern adventure/thriller (quest) novel that is set in Africa (169). In the modern version, expatriates stand for the moral order and have to be rescued in order to preserve that order (171–72). Busia's argument relies on an Africa that is still the Dark Continent in Western eyes: a place of unknown and even unknowable people who cannot understand the ethical practices of an enlightened world and who therefore cannot be relied upon to uphold them.

With the exception of Monsarrat's and possibly Butler's novels, however, this assumption does not hold for Botswana. While Monsarrat and Butler clearly depict a Botswana in which self-destruction is always imminent—either at the hands of the primitive natives or in the awe-inspiring and overpowering wilderness—most of the adventure novels that take place in Botswana seem to be set here in order to take advantage of one of Botswana's most famous features: its peaceful democracy. In Botswana, democracy and the rule of law do not need to be established; they need rather to be preserved: if the people can at least set up a democracy, of course they cannot be expected to preserve it.

A survey of contemporary adventure literature yields a surprising number of novels set in Botswana. The first of these, after Verne, are Nicholas Monsarrat's *The Tribe That Lost Its Head* and its sequel *Richer Than All His Tribe*; both take place on a fictional island off the coast of Namibia that is clearly meant to refer to Botswana, and is equally clearly based on Monsarrat's experiences in the Bechuanaland Protectorate during the crisis of leadership that ensued when Seretse Khama, heir to the BaNgwato chieftainship, married Ruth Williams, a white Englishwoman. Monsarrat's imagined future for Botswana is quite a bit more brutal than what actually unfolded, but his conception of conflict has echoed throughout the adventure stories that subsequently have been set in Botswana. The novels considered here also display common characteristics of the genre: a clear distinction between good and evil, limited character development, and a conservative moral structure. With the exception of Christopher Sherlock's *Night of the Predator*, none of the novels questions the status quo or the ruling elite in its explorations of Botswana's wilderness.

Why does Botswana capture the adventure imagination? Undoubtedly, Botswana's wilderness—both desert and bush—is still wild. In addition, Botswana's peaceful history probably makes it an ideal location for fictional problems: since readers know that revolutions set here cannot be allusions to any real events, it probably seems like an ideal place to make something horrible happen because of the dramatic possibilities in the idea of a peaceful place being destabilized. Finally, Botswana is largely desert, with many people living along the eastern corridor, where there is more reliable water. There are exceptions, of course; nevertheless, traveling in Botswana can give the illusion of being in an empty, dangerous wasteland.

Nicholas Monsarrat was information officer in the British diplomatic service in Johannesburg during the crisis of chieftainship that occurred when Seretse Khama married Ruth Williams. In her book *Colour Bar*, Susan Williams quotes from Monsarrat's correspondence during this period, when he had to deal with the press as well as with other problems that arose in the course of Khama's exile from Serowe. Monsarrat's own feelings about the matter seem to contain a note of peevishness and annoyance at the fact that the BaNgwato and Khama and his wife were not cooperating with the British authorities. He expressed annoyance particularly on two occasions: first when the BaNgwato boycotted the meeting with the High Commissioner, Sir Evelyn Baring, calling the boycott "an atrocious personal insult" (qtd. in Williams 138), and lamenting that all the dignitaries had to take off their magnificent uniforms, which were, in any case, too hot. Second, he referred to Seretse as a nuisance during his brief visit to Ruth, and expressed his displeasure at the fact that journalists were more interested in Ruth, who was pregnant, "ignoring official channels," in other words, Monsarrat himself (qtd. in Williams 161). His unpleasant experiences have translated themselves into his two novels based loosely on those events,[1] and they present a country that apparently did not appreciate all that the British did for it.

Monsarrat is best known for a number of other works, especially *The Cruel Sea*, in addition to these two novels. The island country of Pharamaul off the coast of Namibia (still South-West Africa in the novel) is rather thinly disguised as pre- and postindependence Botswana. Many of the references are

---

1. This is despite his disclaimer in the "Foreword" to *The Tribe That Lost Its Head* that "None of its characters portrays any 'real life' person whatsoever, either living or dead." Readers should be warned about taking such statements, necessary for legal purposes, too literally.

obvious. First, the structure of the words in the languages is similar: "maula" is the root, like "tswana," so that *Phara*maul alludes to *Bot*swana, and includes both the Maulas of the south and the U-Maulas ("not Maulas") of the north. The traditional greeting in Pharamaul is "Ahsula," meaning rain, and the traditional Botswana greeting "Pula" also means rain. The chief is called "barena" and is clearly based on the Sotho-Tswana word for chief *morena*.[2] Second, the U-Maulas resent the Maulas and their social and political power, much as the Kalanga of the north of Botswana resent the status of the BaNgwato. Third, Pharamaul, like Botswana, is vaguely divided into northern and southern regions, connected by a railway corridor in the east, with the capital Port Victoria (Gaborone) in the far south, Gamate (Serowe) in the middle, and Shebiya (Francistown) in the north. Shebiya is where the fish-eating people live, and *bajatlhapi* is a term in Botswana for people from the north who live on or near water and who do, in fact, eat fish.

In *The Tribe That Lost Its Head*, Pharamaul's chief Dinamaula returns from his studies in London to take up his chieftainship, but is forced into exile and eventually "takes up" with a white woman, recalling Seretse Khama's marriage to Ruth Williams and his return from England. *The Tribe That Lost Its Head* is thus a loose retelling of events in the Bechuanaland Protectorate during the 1950s, perhaps rewritten a bit to thoroughly discredit Seretse Khama, but with some of the atrocities of the Mau-Mau in Kenya added for thrills. *Richer Than All His Tribe* (1968) deals, as the title suggests, with the betrayal of

---

2. The more common term for chief in Setswana is *kgosi*, while *morena* is a more general term of address for a superior (in the army as well as in other social situations), as well as being used to refer to the Lord. During the Protectorate period, *morena* was also used to refer to white officials. In Sesotho, however, *morena* (plural *barena*) refers to both chief and the Lord.

Pharamaul's independence by its prime minister Dinamaula, the exiled chief of the first book, whose regime becomes just another corrupt and failed African state.

Both novels repeat a number of familiar stereotypes about the empty beauty of the land and about the backwardness of the "natives." When David Bracken, the protagonist of both novels, makes his first trip to the interior of Pharamaul to visit the other administrators, he only develops affection for the place when he looks at the vastness:

> All he had to fall in love with was this near-deserted siding set in the middle of a brown, dusty plain: some goats, some peering children: a white engineer coming out of a frame house: the sun climbing the sky; and a railway line leading north into the haze, and south into a shadowy blankness, as far as the eye could reach. There was some gritty coffee to cheer him, an off-duty fireman to smile at: the splash of water from the rusty water-tower: a dog sniffing at a thorn tree, a million ants crawling and hurrying on their pathway of destruction. That was all there was, to a dawn in Pharamaul; and yet the moment had a beauty and a simple entrancement that left him breathless. (*The Tribe That Lost Its Head* 90)

Here Monsarrat creates the compellingly beautiful but still slightly menacing imagery that becomes familiar from such later novels as *A Desert of Salt* and others of this type. There are hardly any people here; mostly there are ants "on their pathway of destruction," foreshadowing the eventual and inevitable destruction of Pharamaul itself by its own people.

Additionally, Monsarrat unashamedly reiterates the mythology of the nobility of the colonial enterprise, in which men from England suffer countless hardships and "servitude" in order to bring order to chaotic primitive life in other parts of the world (an order that in a neo-colonial world must still be protected and propped up):

He talked, watched, wandered at will through this curious town which was unlike anything he had ever seen before; he learned the pattern of administration, the delicate balances of care and discipline that kept a backward people happy, the sense of hope and order that made people like Andrew Macmillan, and Forsdick, and Captain Crump, and Llewellyn the agricultural officer, content with their lot, even while they cursed their servitude. (93)

The colonial administrators are able to persevere in their unpleasant and difficult job because they believe that they serve a higher purpose, and Monsarrat's novels do not question this belief at all. The beginning of *Richer Than All His Tribe* is full of scenes in which Maulas are faced with modern life and cannot cope with it: they are incapable of understanding how to vote; they go naïvely into a bank to demand money from their newly independent country, having been told that it all belongs to them now, and cannot understand that they have to put money into an account before they can take it out. Clearly, according to Monsarrat, these people are not yet ready to govern themselves, and these scenes are a consequence of what he perceived as a lack of gratitude on the part of the Batswana during his tenure in the Bechuanaland Protectorate.

Monsarrat's vision of postindependence Botswana—indeed of all postindependence African states—is rather more like a white nightmare. It is replete with unspeakable atrocities committed against the "beneficent" colonial officials who wish only to help the colonies achieve their independence. That independence will then inevitably be squandered by the ungrateful natives. The novels are full of bizarre, fantastical, and somehow weirdly amusing incidents leading up to the rebellion (possibly the "best" one is in *The Tribe That Lost Its Head*, when initiates into the new religion in the north of Pharamaul have a young, beautiful woman give them a hand job so that they ejaculate into the mouth of a dead fish).[3] It seems regrettable that Monsarrat, who had written acclaimed novels, let his resentment find expression in this way.

Ultimately, because of these failings, Monsarrat's novels are less memorable than those that came after, the first of which is K. R. Butler's *A Desert of Salt*, published in 1964. The story takes place in the area north and east of Ghanzi, a supply town in the western part of Botswana, more or less in the middle of the vast desert that crosses from Botswana into Namibia. Many San groups live around the area, working as laborers on the huge cattle ranches owned by settler farmers (Ghanzi is one of the few areas in Botswana where settler farming can be found). Butler's descriptions of the desert and the pans are admiring and respectful. However, whereas in Monsarrat the people are actively portrayed as violent and stupid, and his novels rely on offensive stereotypes, in Butler the people are practically nonexistent.

In *A Desert of Salt*, the world of the Kalahari and of Botswana is an empty hell. Butler's protagonist, Steve Manning, is a veterinary inspection officer of some sort. The story begins with Manning on his way back from inspecting some cattle for lung disease. The owner of the cattle is not identified; the existence of any other person would taint the picture of emptiness that the novel works so hard to create. Here are the first two sentences: "Night was all around me, and yet it was still hot—the heat of the desert between Ghansi and Tukuruku, northwestern Bechuanaland. Heat soaked in through the open windows of the truck and mixed in with the smell of hot metal

---

3. David Maughan-Brown points out in his discussion of Wilbur Smith's novel *Rage* that the Mau-Mau ideology has been used frequently to fan white fears of "native" uprisings (149): this statement is certainly true about Monsarrat's two novels.

and grease" (5). The narrator is alone in the night. He expects it to be cool, as desert nights often are, but it is not. He is sitting in an oven: he can smell the "hot metal and grease." He is fighting a losing battle against his radiator. Looking for water, he finds instead a dead man and his dead dog and a box full of papers chronicling the life of the dead man. The dead man is white, the only inhabitant of this vast, hot, wasteland. Here begins the plot. Although something more dramatic might be expected after such an opening, such as the discovery that he has been killed by "natives," in fact this man has died of loneliness, and his "kaffir bitch" canine companion has conveniently—and faithfully—died with him.

Only when Manning reaches town do any other people—white people—appear, and only after nearly twenty pages the first "boy" appears to take Manning's luggage to his room and to fetch him a beer. The dead man did not keep company with a native woman; Manning, a colonial officer, does not travel with a native assistant; there are no native waiters or mechanics in the town, no native police, in spite of the fact that the Bechuanaland Protectorate employed many Batswana and Basotho police (even Monsarrat's *The Tribe that Lost Its Head* is populated with Batswana police). Butler's story relies on the common, familiar myth of a vast, unpopulated wilderness, where the discoverers must conquer a harsh, unforgiving wasteland and must survive a test of mettle, undertake a journey to prove that "I can do it alone." The appearance of "natives" would imply that the other people routinely cope with this difficult environment; it would also suggest that Manning et al. were not the first ones there. This is one sort of myth that was used to legitimize colonial conquest; it is perhaps somewhat atypical for southern Africa, but it certainly echoes Afrikaner mythology that is based on rights of conquest and occupation versus people who did not occupy the land in a recognizable way. In any case, Butler seems to have bought wholesale into the notion of emptiness, and the suggestion of solitude is quite important to this novel.

However, two of the "natives" in this novel do have names; the most significant one is James, the driver at the head of a convoy going in the opposite direction, from Francistown to Tukuruku; here is where he appears:

> The trucks pulled up to us. There were three of them, loaded with supplies for Tukuruku and beyond, and natives returning from South Africa. The driver of the leading truck was a Bechuana whom I'd run across several times before. He said rather obviously and with a great smile on his fat black face, "I think you are stuck."
>
> I agreed, and asked if his fifty-odd "passengers" could help me out. (50)

Butler, not surprisingly given what has happened so far, presents a stereotype of the stupid, happy African. The passengers are not real people; they are just natives. James himself however is mechanically necessary because he introduces a new white character, one who furthers the conflict and the plot. Manning asks James about a woman who is supposed to be on the convoy but is not:

> He started twisting his feet in the sand, a sure sign he was embarrassed. He said again, "No passenger."
>
> "What happened to her? Did she leave Francistown with you?"
>
> "I think so." "Think" can mean anything to a Bechuana. Maggie might have left with him, or she might not.
>
> "Look, James. Did you have the woman with you when you left Francistown?" He shook his head, which could have been meant for a nod, and told me a long story about leaving Maggie at Kuchu, the last main post on the road before Francistown, some hundred and twenty miles away. At Kuchu there's a decent-size river—usually wet—several huts, a rest house and a petrol pump. It's the biggest settlement along the road. I thought James had got

mixed up between Maggie Roarke and some of his load.
(51–52)

Given that Manning himself cannot tell the difference between "passengers" and a lorry-load, it is not surprising that
he assumes James does the same thing. However, James has
no personality, so he cannot participate in the story—unlike
Manning—he cannot even answer questions. He is just a tool,
a laborer who serves the story by establishing new information.
He has a big smile, and when Manning gives him cigarettes to
distribute to the other drivers, he will keep them all for himself.
This fact is important, even if the man himself is not. He is a
smiling thief;[4] he leaves, without his departure even being no-
ticed: "We were easy meat to them: for one thing, our truck was
lighter; and for another, they weren't having to force us out of
the sand cuts, only straight ahead. Once we were going, there
was no more trouble" (52). The scene ends like that.

The plot thickens, and the characters are now joined by
a beautiful woman, who is looking for the abusive man she
nevertheless loves, and a large, friendly Afrikaner farmer with
his new, bright yellow truck,[5] whose "boy," named Bicycle, also
serves the plot by providing the trigger for revealing the bad
guy (and getting killed in the process). At this point, *A Desert
of Salt* becomes a formulaic adventure story: a safari of whites

---

4. In his story collection *Whites*, Rush includes a story about a young
MoKgalagadi who is also a thief, but not because he wants to steal: "As
from 1978, God chose me for a thief" ("Thieving" 32). He tests God for
putting him in the way of temptation, and so also "starting it" by testing
him.
5. He drives this truck as if it were a team of beloved oxen: "He switched
on and pressed the starter. 'Up you Blouberg; up, now Witvoet; up you
blerry Engeland. There's my beauties. You see how well they pull? Pull
there, you Donker—' He bounced in his seat and cracked an imaginary
whip as the engine started up" (74–75).

in Africa, a search for buried treasure, a murder mystery, using conventional plot rubrics (man against nature, man against man, man against himself). The "natives" function almost as tools to bring all the necessary elements together, and then they are cast aside.

Eliminating the only two named Batswana reinforces the impression of Africa—particularly Botswana—as an uninhabited place: "I remembered that soon we should be running through Motita, a settlement of three or four huts and a thirty-five-foot well which always gave sweet clean water" (44). For Manning, what defines a settlement is huts and water, not the people who occupy the huts. Indeed, Botswana as Butler describes it is simply uninhabitable. The overriding image is one of hell (heat, no water, hot even at night, etc.[6]):

> Towards evening we ran across the northern fringe of the Makarikari. The sun broke through low under the clouds and slanted over the never-ending dead white salt flats. Here and there were patches of raised crust looking like waves of the sea, a white sea that was forever still and silent.... (53–54)

> [W]hen the swamp waters of the north seeped through into the Makarikari, the desert became treacherous. It looked innocent all right, but hidden under the salt crust could be stretches of mud and occasional quicksand.
>
> Frank gave a sort of groan as he stared. "Oh, my God, it hurts. You folks may be used to it, but to me—"
>
> "You must have seen it when you flew over with Johnny."

---

6. Of course, it is important that as a physical description of Botswana's summers, these words are quite accurate. Most people, especially Batswana themselves, probably do not think of Botswana as a hell, however.

"There's a difference between flying over a thing and being in it. Feeling it crush you to pieces." (54)

In this passage, the desert is dangerous, "treacherous" and a place of "neverending" death: even the image of the sea is made to seem dead, "forever still and silent." The image of hell is reinforced when one character describes another's face as "look[ing] like something out of Dante's *Inferno*" (126).[7] This is not a place for "real" living human beings. The suffering of Dante's hell becomes the painfulness of the landscape, and the difficulty of living with it, on it.

The real Kalahari desert is full of people, even in places that look desolate and barren. But in this safari fantasy, this particular hell can only be inhabited—or at least survived—by whites. Butler shows little awareness of the people and has correspondingly little to say about them, and in this aspect as well as in the adventure plot, the novel is not very remarkable. What makes *A Desert of Salt* interesting are precisely the descriptions of the landscape: the painful beauty of the pans.

*The Evil Damp* (1966) is Butler's second novel, also set in Botswana, this time in the Okavango Delta. In this novel, however, the Batswana have more or less disappeared. The occasional "cook-boy" or "native" appears in order to carry a message, and the one named Motswana character, Ndhlovu, is "an insolent rogue, a liar and a thief, but the only boy I'd ever employed who knew how to handle crocs; who was able to look ahead and plan the next move—a characteristic almost nonexistent in Africans" (34).

The narrator, Burt Langford, is a professional hunter, but has not been to this part of the Okavango for two years, during which time many things have changed. Three white couples

---

7. The reference is interesting, although Dante's Hell is as much a place of cold and ice as of fire.

have moved to this location, a kind of camp settlement, and there has been a murder. The real story about the murder does not become clear until the end of the novel, when we learn that one of the white couples of the settlement has committed murder in order to cover up their secret recruitment of "natives" from South-West Africa to join the Communist rebellion there. Langford does not approve of the "filthy theories" (218) of these communist agents, nor does he approve of their method of getting recruits: the Dillons are thought by the Africans to have a very powerful White Magic, and they go to them in order to have their problems solved. The Dillons then blindfold and gag them, submerge them to the chest in quicksand, suspending them by their arms from trees at the edge of the quicksand. Langford understands the effect this treatment can have, because in the Okavango, the "damp black air hugs you closer and closer" (16–17) until an overpowering, mad longing for movement and noise and light sets in. Langford recognizes the cruelty of the Dillons' treatment, and can understand how someone subjected to that torture would be willing to agree to anything in order to be out of isolation.

Langford's inept attempts to get to the bottom of the odd behavior of the settlers at the camp are unconvincing and the anticommunist slant of his narrative perspective, while reflective of the era, is too pedantic for this book to be even as interesting as *A Desert of Salt*. Even the descriptions of the swamps are not as convincing as the descriptions of the pans. We are told that the swamp is beautiful, but not much more is said about it: there is "a secret lagoon, spread over with waxy mauve lilies and bordered by reeds and papyrus and hippo grass" (8), and it "never seemed to vary. It had always been as I was seeing it now: wide, unruffled and beautiful" (18). The idea of recruiting refugees from South-West Africa undoubtedly has a basis in the historical situation (even if the method is somewhat strange): many refugees from the racist states in Rhodesia, South-West Africa, and South Africa passed through or settled in Botswana during the period in which the novel is set. *The Evil Damp* also prefigures later adventure novels, in which Botswana becomes the staging ground for violent political action.

The same image of Botswana as nearly unbearable hell that we see in *A Desert of Salt* also opens Christopher Sherlock's *Night of the Predator* (1991). The prologue describes how the protagonist Max Loxton was saved as an infant by traditional "Bushmen" practices, and how his savior was punished and killed by his father, but the first chapter begins with the following sentences: "The sun was merciless. It beat through the tinted windscreen and the Zeiss lenses of his sunglasses. When he switched off the air-conditioner and opened the side window, the wind came in with a roar and he drank in the hot parched air" (7). Loxton here is driving through Botswana, "pushing two tons of metal…in the burning heat" (7), and contemplating his plans for saving the wildlife of Botswana. It is a labor—the Land Rover is again pushing—but it is a labor of love, for a place. The heat is so powerful that it penetrates both the windscreen and Loxton's wealth in the form of his Zeiss sunglasses. The car contains the plans for Loxton's dream, and he is on his way to meet people who will help make that dream happen: Max Loxton wants "to turn Botswana into a giant game farm" (8)

*Night of the Predator* is mainly about South Africa, but the novel is interesting for its image of Botswana as game farm. The references to Botswana again emphasize the landscape, at the expense of the people who live there. This novel does attempt to be more sensitive to the political struggles of the people than does *A Desert of Salt*, but this story is nevertheless about a desire to protect Botswana from its own people, except of course the Bushmen who saved Loxton's life and who gave him his spiritual compass. Sherlock echoes a powerful attitude here that there is something noble, "ancient," and wise about the San,[8] based on what they are perceived to represent that is in opposition to the rest of the people of Botswana. Sherlock, like many writers of this genre, romanticizes the San at the expense of other groups, whose subsistence farming practices, so he believes, will destroy the land. So Loxton dreams of saving Botswana by making it one giant game park.

Sherlock's novel is classified as political fantasy, and it is very fantastical novel. It is a political thriller that brings together elements from the arms and mining industries and covers a wide range of issues important to the region during the 1980s: tourism, Afrikaner mythology, white supremacy, South Africa's policy of destabilization, resistance to the apartheid government, biological warfare, domestic violence, and corporate interests. In his struggle to preserve Botswana's wildlife, if not its people, Loxton finds himself pitted against powerful political forces in South Africa, including his own father, who is an arms dealer and a member of the apartheid South African government. Loxton's dream for preserving Botswana, with a large hotel/entertainment complex reminiscent of Sun City in the middle of the Okavango Delta (including a below-ground dining area with underwater game viewing), is represented as a noble and worthwhile endeavor.[9]

The background to Loxton's attempt is the political turmoil of South Africa in the 1980s and early 1990s. All sorts of forces are at work to keep the townships destabilized, including

---

8. See for example Laurens van der Post.
9. During the late 1960s and early 1970s, a number of theories put forth the idea that pastoralism was, among other things, destructive of the land that needed to be conserved. Such theories began to be discredited in the late 1970s. Sherlock appears to be drawing on them, but ignores also the problems that people encounter with respect to wildlife (e.g., elephants' destruction of cultivated fields in search of food).

mass media interests from the United States and an unnamed woman who lives in a cave outside of Pietersburg. The novel is in effect a grab-bag of allusions and references to ideas and theories, incidents, and people of South Africa and the world. David Loxton is the terrible Father, industrialist man of steel with a heart to match, power-hungry and ambitious; Max Loxton is his son, the protagonist who wants to "save" Botswana; Victoria Loxton, Max's sister, is a human rights lawyer in Johannesburg, and Lucinda Loxton is Max's other sister, who was sexually abused by her father (thus introducing the problem of domestic violence) but who nevertheless finds brief happiness in an utterly romantic marriage to an English nobleman. Dolph Klopper (perhaps modeled on Eugene ter'Blanche[10]) is the leader of the Afrikaners who is named for Adolf Hitler (Dolph's father was an SS officer and attends a yearly reunion in Vienna with his former colleagues); Kobus van der Post (F. W. de Klerk) is the Afrikaner politician who wants to bring peaceful change to South Africa, and Napoleon Zwane (Nelson Mandela) is the leader of the African Freedom Council, who has been imprisoned for more than twenty years. John Packard, United States media mogul, destroys Max Loxton's dreams as revenge against Loxton for stealing away his wife; his character is possibly based loosely on Ted Turner, but he certainly represents the power of American money. The woman in the cave seems to be an updated version of Rider Haggard's She-Who-Must-Be-Obeyed (*She*). The African Freedom Council is probably a fictionalized African National Congress, and finally there is Ulrich Klee, secretary general of the United Nations, based on the figure of Kurt Waldheim.

---

10. Founder and head, until his murder, of the Afrikaner Resistance Movement (Afrikaner Weerstandsbeweging, AWB).

*Night of the Predator* is interesting as an alternative history: what would have happened if...the AWB had gained power... de Klerk had not been successful...Mandela had not survived imprisonment and so on (in this scenario, "Mandela" [Napoleon Zwane] is released from prison and immediately—within minutes—assassinated by his *imbongi*, or praisesinger). All of the township violence, indeed absolutely everything here, is orchestrated by the woman in the cave, whose power extends also to completely disrupting the attempts of anyone else, including the government and the African Freedom Council, to bring justice and order to South African society. As a novel that in part describes Botswana, it is an extreme example of the same attitude that *A Desert of Salt* displays: ignorance about the people and what they think coupled with an excessive reverence for the land and wildlife. The question arises of what would happen to the people of the country if Botswana were turned into one giant game park? Perhaps they would find themselves in much the same situation that the San find themselves now: either facing repeated relocation or becoming "game" in their own land.

*Night of the Predator* is also the fantasy of a white man who wants to be part of the new South Africa, but in a more heroic way. Once the chemical weapons are unleashed on Soweto, Max Loxton remains in the township to save as many of its inhabitants as he can. He eventually dies from exposure to the chemicals (in fact, he returns to Botswana to die as a Bushman), and his legacy is celebrated by the new government, who put up a bust of him in Soweto: "At the end of the street was a huge bust of a man's head, cast in bronze and already darkened by the weather. It looked out to the north, and on the man's face was a look of determination, of almost religious zeal" (370). Cecil Rhodes's greed is now replaced by a conservationist morality: Loxton's zeal is directed toward Botswana, the country that must be the game park. The inscription states that "'*he was a part of our soul. He will be with us always*'" (370), and Malcolm

Zwane, the son of Napoleon and president of the new South Africa, tells Loxton's sister that "you are more a part of this country than most of us who live here" (369). These tributes are deeply ironic, given that Loxton's dream, one that his widow and sister are rebuilding, means ignoring the very people of whom they are ostensibly a part. Botswana is just a playground of South Africa's rich and powerful, just as the real Botswana is dependent on South Africa even today. Ultimately, the place of Botswana in the region seems clear: as a marvelous vacationland for those who can afford it. It must be remembered, of course, that *Night of the Predator* is primarily about South Africa and was probably written during the height of violence in the 1980s, although it was published just as Mandela was released and things began to change, and as such it is an interesting warning about right-wing white agendas and such.

The next writer refers more specifically to the hunters' histories of the area and so draws on two literary traditions: the hunting diary and the political thriller. The British journalist and satirist Nicholas Luard wrote two novels set in Botswana: *Silverback* (1996) and *Bloodspoor* (1977, written under the pseudonym James McVean). The first is only nominally set in Botswana, since much of the action concerns an around-the-world quest to find out the truth about the protagonist's grandfather. In the novel, Colonel Jack Ruthven was a famous adventurer and amateur ornithologist. There is a plan to expose him as a fraud, and so his granddaughter Victoria sets off to find out the truth. Eventually she ends up in Botswana, where she uncovers some unpleasant facts about her beloved grandfather.

*Bloodspoor* has a more interesting approach: although the plot follows a predictable formula (operatives hired to rescue victim kidnapped by rebels planning to take over Botswana), the characters are somewhat unexpected. The dedication suggests that Luard is or was a keen hunter: "With the author's gratitude to Syd Youthed of Gaborone, Botswana—Companion, hunter and expert guide to the great Kalahari Desert." The protagonist of *Bloodspoor* is Jerry Haston, a professional hunting safari guide in Botswana whose license has been revoked because he exceeded his quota of game. The loss of his license means that he will also lose his livelihood, and so he is a vulnerable target for British officials who hire him to free a naturalist kidnapped by South African guerrillas while she is tracking an elusive black leopard. The naturalist, Alison Welborough-Smith, is a beautiful but smart and strong-willed woman who is good friends with the man who has orchestrated her kidnapping: she has agreed to stay in his camp as long as she can continue her work. Haston is only hired unofficially since the British do not want any publicity; neither do they want a bloodbath, and Haston has a reputation as an excellent tracker. Eventually, things work themselves out in a predictable fashion: Haston and the naturalist begin an affair; the terrorists are killed, as are Haston's hired and expendable Batswana help—whose expertise and skill Haston never fails to praise— and the evil South African government is outwitted in its attempt to discredit the terrorists.

The leopard's power—part of the story is told from his perspective during his trek north, driven to find a mate—becomes here a symbol for the power and danger of the Kalahari Desert, which ultimately cannot be conquered. At the end, only Haston and the naturalist remain; they have seen the elusive leopard, and they are anxious "to go home" (276), the same home of Emily's mother in *Dreams of the Kalahari*. They turn not toward the Delta, where Welborough-Smith has been tracking the leopard, but "towards a motor launch whose prow was glistening *white* in the *darkening* air between the swaying papyrus" (277, emphasis added). The last chapter, like the first, belongs to the leopard, who survives and who rules the dangerous wilderness, thus demonstrating that hunting—and conquest?—is the way to deal with Botswana.

The last three novels are more generic in their use of the place Botswana. Wilbur Smith, born in Rhodesia and familiar with the region, is a well-known writer of southern Africa, having written a number of adventure thrillers and family sagas set in South Africa itself. His novel *The Sunbird* (1972) concerns the popular legend of a lost city of the Kalahari, reputed to be the site of an ancient and magnificent civilization. At the beginning of this novel, Dr. Benjamin Kazin, an archeologist, is shown some aerial photos taken by a friend, who is the head of one of the richest companies in the world. This friend, Lauren Sturvesant, is himself an amateur archaeologist fascinated by the legend of the Lost City. Sturvesant places his unlimited resources at Kazin's disposal, and they go off to Botswana in search of the ruins of the city. Not surprisingly, complications arise in the form of a curse that the ancient inhabitants placed on the site, as well as terrorist activity in the area and encounters with Bushmen, the mysterious and revered experts of the bush. Botswana is a convenient neighbor for South Africa, a useful staging ground for political intrigue, and a place where archeological fantasy can run unbridled.

The remaining two adventure thriller novels set in Botswana use the popular understanding of Botswana as a "haven of democracy" and a stable, peaceful country in order to embellish the story and exaggerate the threat to democracy in southern Africa. Both of them concern special forces who are brought quietly into Botswana in order to preserve it as an oasis of democracy and stability. Steve White's novel *Battle in Botswana* is one of a series about a fictional "S-COM", or Strategic Commando. In this novel, rebels in the Okavango Delta are threatening the "wobbly African democracy" of Botswana, and S-COM, "the mercenary band that dares to deliver," is hired to defeat or "remove" them (according to the blurb on the back of the book). This is a short, quick novel, much like the surgical strike that saves Botswana's "wobbly" government.

Jeff Rovin's *Mission of Honor* is part of a series developed by Tom Clancy[11] and Steve Pieczenik about a special group of commandos who do undercover work for the United States government. In this techno-thriller, a Catholic priest is kidnapped by rebels in Botswana who want their society to return to traditional beliefs. Agents from the "Op-Center" are brought in by Vatican security and the United States government to rescue the priest and resolve the crisis, but they soon discover that the situation is being orchestrated by external forces based in Belgium, who want to gain control of the country's diamond wealth, and who are themselves controlled by a shadowy figure in Japan.

One aspect of *Mission of Honor* that deserves mention is an unexpected consideration of the line between respecting other beliefs and stopping illegal behavior. The head of Op-Center, Paul Hood, finds himself having "to fight a sense of condescension. The fact that this was not his world or set of beliefs should not make it invalid" (203–4), and later he must be reminded again by one of his subordinates that different beliefs do not indicate insanity:

> "He's [Thomas Burton, leader of the Vodunists in Botswana] still hearing voices in some fashion," Hood said. "You consider that sane?"
>
> "You mentioned Moses a minute ago," the woman replied. "What makes you think that Thomas Burton is any less rational? How do you know he is not what he says?"
>
> Hood wanted to answer, *Common sense.* But something in Liz's voice made him hesitate. Her tone was not critical of Hood but respectful of Thomas Burton....
>
> Hood felt a flush of shame. Liz had been right to ask

---

11. Tom Clancy apparently had an abiding fascination for Jules Verne. See William F. Ryan, "The Genesis of the Techno-Thriller."

that question. It was not the right of Paul Hood or anyone else to make qualitative judgments about the Vodunists or people of any faith. (205–6)

The consideration demonstrated here toward the figure and motives of Thomas Burton sets the reader up to be sympathetic to his cause, although Burton's status is later undercut when it is revealed that he is just being used without his knowledge by other, more powerful, men with money.

All of the novels discussed here show a certain fascination with the landscape of Botswana, and almost no regard for its people. The desire to protect the "wobbly" democracy conveniently overlooks the fact that the democracy has been maintained for forty years, without any military intervention (at least of the sort envisioned and described). Whether as an empty hell, a game park, a place of mystical wildlife—including the Bushmen—or a wobbly near-democracy, Botswana is still, in the tradition of Rhodes, simply a place that one has to pass through. J. M. Coetzee said in his Jerusalem Prize acceptance speech that "their [white masters of South Africa] talk, their excessive talk about how they love South Africa has consistently been directed toward *the land*…" (97). Even the most unyielding and unforgiving landscape can become a haven of love and peace if the people of the land are respected and loved, as they are for example in Bessie Head's *When Rain Clouds Gather*. Botswana is a physically beautiful—and physically harsh—place, but it is Bo-Tswana: the place of the Tswana.

## LADY DETECTIVES—ALEXANDER MCCALL SMITH
## AND LAURI KUBUITSILE

Mmapula Ditsamaiso, the woman who heads the carjack-ing syndicate in Andrew Sesinyi's *Carjack*, warns Brutus early on that she is not to be messed with, and she is the embodiment of what men seem to fear in a woman: predatory sexuality that cannot be resisted, beautiful, ruthless, and in charge of everything. Her "good-girl" counterpart in fiction about Botswana finds personification in a very unlikely place—or two places, actually: Precious Ramotswe, lady detective creation of Alexander McCall Smith, and Kate Gomolemo, police detective creation of Lauri Kubuitsile, two women who are in fact fearsome—if also sympathetic—when it comes to dealing with the problems of society, as well as the weaknesses of men.

Professional women detectives are a recent phenomenon in literature generally, though amateurs have a long history. Linda Mizejewski observes that they seem to be more common or popular in books than in visual media and argues that this can in part be accounted for by the ambiguous nature of the female detective in books. In order to capture a TV or film audience, lady detectives have to be successful in a more physical way: what makes female detectives so popular in fiction does not translate well into film or TV, since often, visual success requires a more conformist appearance. Kinsey Millhone, for example, of Sue Grafton's alphabet series of crime novels, is never described in any detail; all we know is that she only owns one dress and that she cuts her own hair with nail scissors. However, she is very popular among readers for her somewhat maverick social commentary (Mizejewski 36). Mizejewski's argument focuses of the role of the body (of the detective as well as of the suspects and the corpses) in popular female detective fiction, films, and TV series; more generally, she writes that "[f]or better or for worse, cultural ideas about detectives are wedded to the books, films, and television programs that shape our assumptions about crime investigation…" (Mizejewski 2). They may shape our perceptions about how crime is investigated, but crime investigation novels can tell us something about what a culture values. They are popular fiction in the strictest sense of the term. McCall Smith states that "[i]n mystery or crime fiction you can talk about so much within a society," and his own "mysteries, such as they are, provide a vehicle for portraying the society and the people who live in Botswana" (Silet 29). In a personal message, Lauri Kubuitsile said that she wanted to write "very fast moving, popular fiction looking at the real Botswana issues" (17 October 2006).

Alexander McCall Smith's detective creation Precious Ramotswe is a familiar type of woman in southern Africa. She is not only "traditionally built," she is also somewhat traditionally minded, and takes a very sensible approach to life. She is hardworking, and she recognizes what women like her contribute to the society. She admires her maid Rose,[1] who, in addition to

---

1. It is common for middle-class families in Botswana to have maids.

cleaning Mma Ramotswe's house, takes in sewing to support herself and her three children; "Africa was full of such women, it seemed, and if there was to be any hope for Africa it would surely come from women such as these" (*In the Company of Cheerful Ladies* 10). In one interview, McCall Smith states that "[i]n some African societies women can have quite a difficult time, and because African women are usually very hard-working and resourceful and often very put upon, I thought it would be appropriate to describe the society from that particular angle" (Silet 29). Mma Ramotswe herself, however, is in some ways a maverick in her own society: a woman who starts her own detective business, who does not tolerate male chauvinist nonsense from men but who nevertheless is sensitive to how men feel about things.

Lauri Kubuitsile's Detective Kate Gomolemo is even more of a maverick than Mma Ramotswe. Like Precious Ramotswe, Kate Gomolemo is a strong African woman, perhaps a typical example of the women who take care of, but do not necessarily run, Botswana society. Kubuitsile's own perceptions of Batswana women echo McCall Smith's, but Kubuitsile describes the situation with a finer edge:

> I've always felt Batswana women were exceptionally strong with almost super-hero levels of resilience. I wondered if it didn't come from historically living without men who were at the S[outh] A[frican] mines for many years at a time. In some ways I've often thought the patriarchal nature of Setswana society is a bit of a farce, put on to placate men. In most cases you find that on the surface men may be the bosses but when it comes down to really analysing what is going on there is a strong woman in the mix who is likely doing most everything. (17 October 2006)

The women she describes create a profile that fits Mma Ramotswe quite well, and her own creation Detective Gomolemo less well. Gomolemo is more overtly and obviously in charge, whereas Mma Ramotswe works more by observing and managing human nature. Like the women in Sesinyi's *Carjack*, these are both women who are in control, but this time on the side of the forces of good.

Alexander McCall Smith's novels are enjoying huge popularity in the West. He himself seems a little bemused by this popularity, noting that he originally wrote the first novel as a short story: "It started off as a short story, it became a book, and then I discovered suddenly that I was writing a whole series of books" (Mekgwe 180). *The No. 1 Ladies' Detective Agency* has been translated into thirty-one languages, and it has the distinction of being assigned reading for some undergraduate courses in African literature in the United States.

Therein, however, lies part of the controversy surrounding the novels: McCall Smith's novels have started to be read as representative of African literature. His nostalgic, romanticized view of the country and people of Botswana is read, not surprisingly, as typical of the paternalistic approach that characterizes much of the West's interaction with the people and societies of Africa. Africa is often understood in the West to be a place of disease, war, poverty, starvation, and death. In *Tears of the Giraffe*, an American woman who hires Mma Ramotswe to find out what happened to her son more than ten years ago summarizes these preconceptions about Africa:

> "I came to Africa twelve years ago. I was forty-three and Africa meant nothing to me. I suppose I had the usual ideas about it—a hotchpotch of images of big game and savannah and Kilimanjaro rising out of the cloud. I also thought of famines and civil wars and potbellied, half-naked children staring at the camera, sunk in hopelessness. I know that all that is just one side of it—and not the most important side either—but it was what was in my mind." (25)

This theme recurs, almost like a *leitmotif,* in a number of the other novels—*Morality for Beautiful Girls* (27), *In the Company of Cheerful Ladies* (4), and especially in *Blue Shoes and Happiness*: "*If only more people knew,* thought Mma Ramotswe. *If only more people knew that there was more to Africa than all the problems they saw. They could love us too, as we love them*" (128, italics in original).

Certainly this is true, and it is true of probably every place on earth,[2] and McCall Smith himself has said that

> [a]lso I think it's a great pity that when people think about Africa these days they think about the images of starvation, AIDS, and suffering—which admittedly are a part of the reality of Africa—but they are only one part of the reality. People never hear about the decency, the humor, the warmth, the human niceness of so many people in Africa. I would hope these books can try to do something in a small way about portraying some marvelous human values and qualities, to try perhaps to correct the overly sad picture of Africa we get. People are frightened of Africa.... (Silet 30)

So these novels are less about crime and more about the people of a particular place and how they live and get on with their lives. The fact that they are about people's lives is central to enjoying them, and concern for people's lives is also central to Mma Ramotswe's approach to her work.

The underlying issue, in most of the cases that Mma Ramotswe deals with, is a moral one. McCall Smith "find[s] these moral issues interesting" (Mekgwe 182); in his professional life he studies and writes about bio-ethical problems in law and medicine. In another interview, he says that *The No. 1 Ladies' Detective Agency* "is not a terribly conventional mystery. There

---

2. A cleric from Iran who once visited the United States expressed surprise at the number of churches he saw.

is not a great deal of actual crime, and it's fairly incidental to the other problems that Mma Ramotswe deals with" (Silet 29). She does not like to investigate crimes, because she knows that is the job of the police force. Mma Ramotswe refers to her work more as solving problems than solving crimes, and most of what she does is summarized neatly for the readers in *Blue Shoes and Happiness*, when she considers the possibility of organizing her case files by subject: "There would be a large file for adultery....There could be a section for suspicious husbands and one for suspicious wives, perhaps, and even one for male menopause cases now that she came to think about it. Many of the women who came to see her were worried about their middle-aged husbands..." (30). Morality appears in many different guises—Why do some men cheat on their wives? Why do some women marry for money? Why do some people try to defraud others?—and in a more general way, Mma Ramotswe laments the passing of the society she knew when she was a child, the loss of the old ways.

The clash between old and new moralities is perhaps a second *leitmotif* that runs through the novels. In its most basic form, this clash is represented by the figures of the two apprentice mechanics who work for Mr. J. L. B. Matekoni, Mma Ramotswe's fiancé. They seem incapable of taking their work seriously, and Mma Makutsi, Mma Ramotswe's assistant, is convinced that they only ever think about girls. Mma Ramotswe thinks frequently in this environment about the problem of morality, and she defines it for the first time in *Morality for Beautiful Girls*:

> It occurred to Mma Ramotswe that such [unkind] behaviour was no more than ignorance; an inability to understand the hopes and aspirations of others. That understanding, thought Mma Ramotswe, was the beginning of all morality. If you knew how a person was feeling, if you could imagine yourself in her position, then surely it would be impossible to inflict further pain. (75)

This understanding seems to be lacking in the modern life, personified by the apprentices, that she must deal with in her work. Every novel after this one contains a reference to that lack as she encounters it in her work:

> If you woke up one day and thought that you might find somebody more exciting than the person you had, then you could walk out!...Where had all this come from, she wondered. It was not African, she thought, and it certainly [had] nothing to do with the old Botswana morality. (*The Kalahari Typing School for Men* 120)

> The modern world was selfish, and full of cold and rude people. Botswana had never been like that, and Mma Ramotswe was determined that her small corner of Botswana...would always remain part of the old Botswana, where people greeted one another politely and listened to what others had to say, and did not shout or think just of themselves. (*The Full Cupboard of Life* 6–7)

> It was not true that such a thing could not have happened in the old Botswana—it could—but it was undoubtedly true that this was much more likely to happen today. There were many selfish people about these days, people who seemed not to care if they scraped the cars of others or bumped into people while walking on the street. Mma Ramotswe knew that this was what happened when towns became bigger and people became strangers to one another; she knew, too, that this was a consequence of increasing prosperity, which , curiously enough, just seemed to bring out greed and selfishness. But even if she knew why all this happened, it did not make it any easier to bear. (*In the Company of Cheerful Ladies* 2)

> But there was nothing in the old Botswana morality which said that one could not forgive those who were weak; indeed, there was much in the old Botswana morality that

was very specifically about forgiveness. (*Blue Shoes and Happiness* 101)

Thus, Mma Ramotswe, although she does not solve big crimes, does in fact consider the rightness or wrongness of the behavior of people she deals with. In a longer consideration of the changes that modern Botswana society is facing because of its increased prosperity, Mma Ramotswe recognizes that "[l]ife was far better...if we knew who we were" (*In the Company of Cheerful Ladies* 3), implying that modern life brings a loss of self-knowledge, self-awareness, and self-identity.[3] Knowing who you are makes you aware of the relationships that bind you to other people, and for Mma Ramotswe this means the relationships that bind her to Botswana. These relationships make it impossible for someone to dent another's car in a parking lot and then just drive away (the observation of which prompts her to consider the nature of these relationships) because if it is possible that you know this person, then why would you ignore someone you know?

---

3. Interestingly, in his address to open Parliament on 13 November 2006, President Festus Mogae specifically referred to the growing materialism of Botswana society and to the effect that it was having:

> Mr. Speaker, whilst I readily accept that it is the right of every citizen to reward himself or herself for their lifelong struggles, I feel the obligation, as one of the elder citizens, to plead that we should not abandon our traditional modesty. There is no doubt that some of the unfortunate incidents such as suicides and the disturbing crime rate are indicative of the rising social stress levels and loss of values resulting from the pursuit of ostentatious lifestyles.
>
> I am also concerned, like other fellow citizens, that unless we arrest our current pursuit of consumerist lifestyles, we will distort our national value system and begin to judge people only by their meretricious sparkle and superficial looks rather than by the intrinsic value of the content of their character. (paras. 94–95)

In a more general way, this moral consideration underlies all of the novels. One can almost hear McCall Smith, in the voice of Precious Ramotswe, asking his readers how they can make such harsh judgments about a place they have never been to see? About whose people they know nothing? When in fact we all worry about the same things? When an American woman asks Mma Ramotswe to stand in a picture with her friend, Mma Ramotswe quickly agrees and

> felt [the other woman's] arm against hers, flesh against flesh, warm and dry as the touch of human flesh so often and so surprisingly is. She had sometimes thought that this is what snakes said about people: *and, do you know, when you actually touch these creatures they aren't slimy and slippery, but warm and dry?* (*Blue Shoes and Happiness* 129)

McCall Smith, with these novels, seems to ask his readers to do what all good literature asks its readers to do: to consider things from someone else's point of view.

But the fact remains that McCall Smith's are not African novels in the commonly defined way. The misperception that he somehow writes on behalf of Africa hinders more sensible reception of his books. The books do not offer complicated social insights about contemporary African society and the tangled origins of current problems. He writes about Botswana as an outsider, but nevertheless he writes as one whose view is not limited to the painful desert, or indeed to any painful aspect. He does not write overtly about AIDS, for example, and he has been roundly criticized for ignoring this problem. He does, in fact, refer to AIDS, but in the way that people in Botswana frequently talk about it: in an oblique manner, not mentioning the disease by name, but recognizing that it is always there, between funerals, and in the suffering of so many family members. At one point in *In the Company of Cheerful Ladies*, for example, when Mma Ramotswe and her family attend Sunday morning service at the Anglican Cathedral, she hears a sermon by Bishop Trevor Mwamba (a real person), in which he talks about the suffering of AIDS victims without ever mentioning the disease. The final paragraph of his sermon summarizes beautifully how many people in Botswana cope with the literally indescribable burden:

> If we look about our world today, if we look about this dear home of ours, Africa, then what do we see but tears and sorrow? Yes we see those. We see those even in Botswana, where we are so fortunate in many ways. We see those in the faces of those who are ill, in their fear and their sorrow at the thought that their lives will be so shortened. This is real suffering, but it is not suffering that we as Christians walk away from. Every day, every moment of every day, there are people who are working to alleviate this suffering. They are working at this task right now as I speak, right across the road in the Princess Marina Hospital.[4] There are doctors and nurses working. There are our own people and generous-hearted people from far way, from America, for example, who are working here to bring relief to those who are very sick from this cruel illness that stalks Africa. Do those people talk about such suffering as proof that there can be no divine presence in this world? They do not. They do not ask that question. And many are sustained by that very faith at which some clever people like to sneer. And that, my friends, is the true mystery at which we should marvel. That is what we should think about in silence for a moment, as we remember the names of those who are ill, those members of this body, this Anglican church, our brothers and sisters. And I read them out now. (31–32)[5]

---

4. Princess Marina is the main government hospital in Gaborone, and it is also the center for AIDS research and treatment in the country.
5. Some of Bishop Mwamba's sermons have been collected in *Dancing Sermons*.

In this sermon, Mwamba asks his parishioners for the same kind of understanding that is the foundation of Mma Ramotswe's morality. He does not mention AIDS by name; few people do. Most people have to get on with their lives, and so "this cruel illness" is hardly mentioned between funerals. In that aspect, by not talking about AIDS directly, McCall Smith's novels give a very accurate picture of Botswana society. These novels are about something else.

In the sense that McCall Smith seems to be referring to morality, AIDS is not a moral problem; it is a disease. It only becomes a moral problem when we judge people who suffer from it, and when as a result people do not exhibit the understanding that Mma Ramotswe demonstrates toward all her clients, and that especially Mma Makutsi demonstrates toward her brother Richard, who suffers and eventually dies from AIDS. Numerous characters make reference to the scourge of AIDS (the unmentionable disease) in their society, but they do not live their lives in dreaded anticipation of it or running away from it. It is there, and they must deal with it, and in the meantime others must get on with their lives. McCall Smith seems to avoid referring to linking promiscuity and unfaithfulness to the spread of AIDS when he says that "[p]articularly as an outsider, I don't think it's for me to spend too much time on that particular issue" (Mekgwe 183), but Mma Ramotswe alludes to a moral problem of dishonesty when she considers how the spread of AIDS increases in a society where people are so quick to discard one another. More specifically, Poppy, one of Mma Ramotswe's clients, makes her feelings on the matter quite clear: "'Look at what all this unfaithfulness has done. People are dying because of that, aren't they? Many people are dying'. For a moment the three of them were silent. There was no gainsaying what Poppy had said. It was just true. Just true" (*Blue Shoes and Happiness* 36). The statement raises all sorts of questions about what happens to women whose husbands die "after a long illness": what stigma must she suffer, and what fear blankets her mind? Questions of morality thus take on a very broad cast in the Precious Ramotswe novels.

As Pinkie Mekgwe points out in her interview with McCall Smith, Botswana is a society that is struggling mightily with AIDS and its associated problems. His reply to her comment explains why he does not deal with such problems more overtly: "I think that it is important to be optimistic. I don't really have much time for a nihilistic, denying philosophy of life....So I suppose I am a bit of a utopian novelist. I am not a social realist novel[ist], I am not really concerned with describing things always as they are; rather I look at how they might be" (Mekgwe 183). McCall Smith does not shove Botswana's problems in its face, but, like HIV/AIDS, they are present in the novels. For example, suspicion of and even prejudice against other Africans is quite common in Botswana society: Mma Ramotswe herself believes that Zulus are loud and aggressive (*The Kalahari Typing School for Men* 209), and she imagines that purgatory might be a bit like Nigeria (*Tears of the Giraffe* 5–6). As pointed out earlier, most of Mma Ramotswe's cases deal with cheating spouses, and no one argues when Poppy suggests that unfaithfulness contributes to the spread of AIDS.

McCall Smith should probably not be understood as an African writer, but as a writer from outside Botswana, his focus provides an interesting comparison to other similar writers, such as Rush, Butler, Slaughter, and such. Even in the way he describes the land, McCall Smith is different from most of his predecessors. *The No. 1 Ladies' Detective Agency* starts with an allusion to Isak Dinesen ("I had a farm in Africa, at the foot of the Ngong Hills" [13]): "Mma Ramotswe had a detective agency in Africa, at the foot of Kgale Hill" (1). McCall Smith's narrator is quite different from Dinesen's "I" because the narrator is not at the center of the story, whereas Dinesen's "I" is at the center of her observations about British/Kenyan society and of Gikuyu society, rather like Rush's narrators, who are at the center of their social environments, and whose interest in the rest of the Botswana environment extends only to the point that it tells them something about themselves. Dinesen's narrator speaks from the point of view of one consciously observing a different society, like an anthropologist, like the narrator-protagonist of *Mating*.

A certain irony, too, surfaces in McCall Smith's next sentences, which differ even more startlingly from the description of Dinesen's lush coffee plantation:

> These were [the agency's] assets: a tiny white van, two desks, two chairs, a telephone, and an old typewriter. Then there was a teapot, in which Mma Ramotswe…brewed redbush tea. And three mugs—one for herself, one for her secretary, and one for the client. What else does a detective agency really need? Detective agencies rely on human intuition and intelligence, both of which Mma Ramotswe had in abundance. No inventory could ever include those, of course. (*The No. 1 Ladies' Detective Agency* 1)

The foliage of Dinesen's farm and the beauty of the place are contrasted in *Out of Africa* itself with European forests, but they are contrasted here with Mma Ramotswe's "intuition and intelligence." The most notable feature of Dinesen's farm is the air (13); the most notable feature in McCall Smith's Botswana is the people who live there: Mma Ramotswe, her father Obed, her friend Mr. J. L. B. Matekoni, and the other people who come to her for help. A detective story must be about people, and this series of novels has them in abundance.

The discussion of the landscape is also interesting because it is described in terms that specifically reject the notion of ownership ("But there was also the view, which again could appear on no inventory" [1]). Here we see a challenge to the notion of property that is so often used by white settlers writing about their farms, such as Dinesen, who speaks for numerous pages of the view and smell of the land before she even gets to the people who work for her.[6] Botswana here cannot be inventoried and owned, as Emily in *Dreams of the Kalahari* comes to learn; this Botswana changes from the "solitary desert" that she first needs to find her inner peace to a place that does not need to be conquered, as it does in Rush's work, or protected, as it does in *Night of the Predator*. We see this affection for place that is not tarnished by proprietary claims most clearly when Mma Ramotswe's father, Obed, returns from the South African mines:

> When I came home that time, and got off the bus at Mochudi, and saw the *kopje* and the chief's place and the goats, I just stood and cried. A man came up to me—a man I did not know—and he put his hand on my shoulder and asked me whether I was just back from the mines. I told him that I was, and he just nodded and left his hand there until I had stopped weeping. Then he smiled and walked away. He had seen my wife coming for me, and he did not want to interfere with the homecoming of a husband. (*The No. 1 Ladies' Detective Agency* 25)

Obed sees the hill (*kopje*), but he also sees the chief's place (where the community gathers at the *kgotla*), and he is comforted by another man who seems to understand the significance of coming home (or perhaps Home?) after working in the hostile environment of South Africa's mines.

Obed's relief at getting away from all the problems of life in South Africa can be seen in the way the novels themselves blur references to some of the things that characterize modern Botswana: increasing crime, high unemployment, HIV/AIDS, inter-ethnic tension. Obed escapes back to where he was born,

---

6. See pages 13–16, after which she writes "*We* grew coffee on *my* farm" (16, emphasis added).

and in some ways to the time he was born. One of the aspects that distinguishes *The No. 1 Ladies' Detective Agency* from the subsequent novels is the memoir of Obed Ramotswe, in his voice (although he has died before the first novel opens), that takes up several chapters: Obed "worked in the mines of South Africa. He tells of the arrogance of white miners and of the ethnic violence of the compounds, yet prefers to focus on the moments when these were transcended—the Zulu who was his friend, the one white miner he could talk to" (Bennett 43). This memoir establishes the understanding that Mma Ramotswe needs in order to be an effective private detective; it is the understanding that she longs for in others. In effect, Obed chooses to escape from the realities of South Africa to the kinder life of Mochudi (one that probably no longer exists), and in McCall Smith's novels, readers can escape to a place where courtesy matters, where people still look out for each other, where men and women marry for reasons other than looks or money. The novels are not real life: "Real life…isn't like that. But we suspend our disbelief because McCall Smith makes such a convincing case that…it just might be" (Robinson 4).

Thus the novels are about humanity (*botho*[7]), and Mma Ramotswe is hardly, unlike Dinesen, a detached observer. As she observes at one point, when she is combing the newspapers for gossip, she "could not understand people who took no interest in all this. How could one live in a town like this and not want to know everybody's business, even if one had no professional reason for doing so?" (223). The concern of the novel is what people do and how they go about their lives. Of course, this business of knowing other people's affairs cuts two ways, but

---

7. *Botho* is a Setswana word that refers to the common experience of being human; it is generally considered in a positive sense, like the more familiar *ubuntu*.

Mma Ramotswe is interested because she wants to help them solve their problems; it is her *business*.

Because these novels are not simply detective or crime novels, because they are about the human character and the moral choices we face—set in the particular society Botswana—it is not surprising, then, to discover, that many of the characters are based on people McCall Smith has met here.[8] Robinson describes them as "true stories of fictional people" (4). McCall Smith's own optimism becomes superimposed onto people whose lives might not be as cheerful as they would like, but could be as cheerful as he can make them. The people that McCall Smith met in Botswana are those whom he met in 1981, before the strong desire for material wealth took hold and when the "old morality" of people like Mma Ramotswe's father Obed still governed the behavior of most people. One of the reasons that the novels seem so naïvely optimistic and even paternalistic today is that the Botswana McCall Smith describes is fading further and further into remote villages. Real life, in Gaborone today, is less and less like the world that McCall Smith has created for Mma Ramotswe and her family and friends; in the novels "Botswana comes through as being

---

8. Precious Ramotswe herself is based on a woman McCall Smith once met who caught and killed a chicken; the two orphans are based on real case files at the SOS Children's Village (see Robinson). Some of the real-life characters who appear are Bishop Trevor Mwamba, the former Anglican archbishop of Botswana, Dr. and Mrs. Moffat, and McCall Smith himself, who appears in a photograph that Mrs. Moffat shows to Mma Ramotswe:

> "That is somebody who comes to stay with us from time to time," said Mrs Moffat. "He writes books."
>
> Mma Ramotswe examined the photograph more closely. "It seems that he is looking at me," she said. "He is smiling at me."
>
> "Yes," said Mrs Moffat. "Maybe he is." (*The Kalahari Typing School for Men* 176–77)

the hero, yes" (Mekgwe 183), but it is the Botswana that is lamented by Sesinyi and Baruti, who desire a return to the old ways. Modern Botswana just is not like that any more. Mma Ramotswe knows that, and there are probably things about that past that she would rather did not return: "[S]he says that she admires the old Botswana ways and often tut tuts a bit about some modern behaviour. She is, though, selective in the old values that she likes" (Mekgwe 185). Still, she regrets, over and over, the passing of courtesy and understanding—*botho*.

If Mma Ramotswe shows us the good possibilities of real life, then Lauri Kubuitsile's novels show the nasty possibilities of real life, in a more conventional crime/thriller style. Kubuitsile writes with the deliberate attempt to provide escape: "Though I'm quite political by nature, I think African literature must lighten up. Not everything must be literary and political. Let's have fun!"[9] Kubuitsile, when asked whether her novel offered an alternative to the Mma Ramotswe novels, replied that she "didn't really think about [McCall Smith] at all, I don't think the books are of the same nature" (17 October 2006). *The Fatal Payout* introduces a detective in the Botswana Criminal Investigation Department (CID), Kate Gomolemo. It is a short novel, but contains references to many of the issues that confront Batswana at the start of the twenty-first century: rising crime, the belief in the tradition of rags-to-riches, rampant materialism, sexual abuse in the workplace, HIV/AIDS, extramarital affairs, expatriate (often South African) perceptions that Botswana is "easy pickings", the rise of so-called passion killings,[10]

---

9. Of course, there is a great deal of African literature that is much lighter than what Kubuitsile refers to: Macmillan's Pacesetter series comes immediately to mind.

10. "Passion-killing" is a term that has been coined to refer to the murder of someone, usually a woman, by her partner or ex-partner (husband or

promiscuity, and so forth. The story concerns a case of black-mail and murder that touches on all of these issues, represented by various characters: John Mogami is a man from a very poor, rural background whose wife has become more greedy with Mogami's material success. He is susceptible to bribes because of his wife's greed; he is also susceptible to blackmail by his secretary, who needs money to pay for her antiretroviral medication (she has AIDS). The secretary sleeps around in order to infect as many people as possible, and she is killed. Detective Gomolemo assumes that the boyfriend has killed her because that sort of crime is on the rise. The man who wants to bribe Mogami is a South African who works in Botswana because he finds it easy to bribe government officials to win tenders/bids; he is eventually caught in a trap set by one of his female assistants, who is tired of his constant sexual attention. Finally, Mrs. Mogami loses her husband when she embarks on an affair with a man where she works, who promises to buy her expensive presents.

Kate Gomolemo is only introduced about halfway through the novel: "Kate Gomolemo was an attractive woman, the kind of beauty that only becomes more pronounced with age. But despite being attractive there was a seriousness about her, sadness even" (43). Once she arrives, however, she has an immediate impact. She reads people well (a necessary skill for a detective) and makes them nervous, even fearful. She is smart and emotionally strong, characteristics that she needs in order to sort out the mess that the men have created. In fact, most of the men in this book are weak, ineffectual, or corrupt, to varying degrees. What makes Kate most like Precious, though, is her strong sense of what is right and what is wrong:

---

boyfriend) out of jealousy or possessiveness; the murder is often followed by the suicide of the murderer. The number of these killings rose greatly in the first decade of the twenty-first century.

> She could see that [John Mogami] was troubled....But
> she could also see that he was a good man, a decent man
> who had worked hard to get to where he was; a man with
> character. He was a kindred spirit and she identified with
> him right away. (44)

Gomolemo is able to recognize decency in others because she practices it herself; she has Mma Ramotswe's kind of understanding.

The fact that Kubuitsile raises so many social issues suggests that she too is concerned with or interested in the moral structure of Botswana society. The chief male character in *The Fatal Payout*, John Mogami, wants very badly to do what is right, but he is too weak to stand up to temptation. When he is offered a bribe that will end all his financial problems, he says he will think about it and decide in the morning, "But in his heart, John already knew what that decision would be" (17). However, as light reading, *The Fatal Payout* fills the bill:

> This novel came to be in a very offhand way. We were
> changing the format of our newspaper from tabloid size
> to a smaller A4 advertiser size so that we could print it
> for ourselves. At the time there were a few such papers in
> our market and I wanted to find ways to set us apart from
> others. This is where the idea of a serialised novel came
> in. I wanted it very fast moving, popular fiction looking
> at the real Botswana issues. I thought about *Love On The
> Rocks* when I was writing it. That's what I was shooting for.
> (personal communication, 17 October 2006)

McCall Smith's and Kubuitsile's novels are not meant to carry the weight of "African literature": they represent two people's views about the society that they are, in perhaps only a small way, a part of. Botswana is not just a place of big game[11]

---

11. Abacus, the paperback publisher of the McCall Smith novels has,

and dangerous swamps and desert, and these novels represent the possibility that the West can look at the rest of the world with a bit more sympathy—and even recognition.[12]

---

however, fallen back on those stereotypes to decorate the covers of the books; all their paperback versions feature large drawings of animals: a crocodile (*The No. 1 Ladies' Detective Agency*), a giraffe (*Tears of the Giraffe*), lions (*Morality for Beautiful Girls*), an ostrich (*The Kalahari Typing School for Men*), an elephant (*The Full Cupboard of Life*), a zebra (*In the Company of Cheerful Ladies*), meerkats (*Blue Shoes and Happiness*), and hoopoes (*The Good Husband of Zebra Drive*). The first edition of *The No. 1 Ladies' Detective Agency* featured a photograph of a Motswana woman in front of a traditionally decorated rondavel (hut). Animals appear in the novels, but not with nearly the prominence that they have on the Abacus covers. The Abacus cover of *Blue Shoes and Happiness* is perhaps a bid to cash in on the popularity of the nature soapie "Meerkat Manor." It will be interesting to see what wanders onto the cover of *The Miracle at Speedy Motors*.

At the time of writing, *The No. 1 Ladies' Detective Agency* had just finished filming (under the direction of Anthony Minghella) in Gaborone. Lauri Kubuitsile has completed three more Kate Gomolemo novels, in which she develops the relationship between Gomolemo and Mogami, and in which she tackles some of Botswana's thorniest problems head on; she also won a prestigious South African literary prize in October 2007, the BTA/AngloPlatinum Short Story Prize and the Platinum Prize for Creativity, for her short story "A Christmas Wedding."

12. Grant Lilford comments that it is "disturbing how the West seems so keen to latch on to white writers as spokespeople for Africa—whether Gordimer, Wilbur Smith, Dinesen or McCall Smith—and how it treats black African authors as curiosities to be prescribed in black studies courses, but never to be popular" (message to the author, 2008).

# THE POSSIBILITY OF JUSTICE—BESSIE HEAD
## AND UNITY DOW

> The ancestors made so many errors and one of the
> most bitter-making things was that they relegated to
> men a superior position in the tribe, while women were
> regarded, in a congenital sense, as being an inferior
> form of human life. ("The Collector of Treasures" 92)

Bessie Head and Unity Dow are the first fiction writers from
Botswana to make a name for themselves abroad. The
body of their work is quite substantial: Dow already has four
novels to her name, and will probably continue to write more,
and Bessie Head has five novels, a collection of short stories,
and numerous other nonfiction writings, as well as voluminous
correspondence. Their observations about Botswana society
are quite acute and offer a point of view that is not often seen
in writing by other Batswana. In particular, they look at things
in society from the perspective of the underdog—in Dow's
case, the underdog is unabashedly female; in Head's case, the

underdog is anyone who suffers at the hands of someone with more power. Their novels, while probably not as popular as Alexander McCall Smith's, give a more complex view of the state of Botswana society, and in different ways, they make a case for the cause of social justice.

Both writers are engaged and familiar with Botswana society and customs: Bessie Head from her life but also from her studies of Botswana's history (see discussion of *A Bewitched Crossroad* earlier), and Dow from her work as a human and women's rights activist and as a former justice of the High Court of Botswana.[1] Dow has worked on women's legal issues, and in 2006 wrote an important opinion concerning the relocation of a group of San from the Central Kalahari Game Reserve.[2] Dow and Head write with affection and familiarity, but with a clear understanding of the processes at work among people. They write, but critically, and also in many ways they write hopefully of the future, imagining a Botswana based on what they believe is good about the community.

David Newmarch, in a 1994 article in *Swansea Review*, posits that in the course of Bessie Head's writing, Serowe becomes the focus of her writing life, "the locus of her present experience and the point from which she was impelled to reach back into Southern African history" (440–41). Head creates the locality of Serowe (and, to a degree, Botswana), in much the way that other writers have done; for example, Faulkner's Yoknapatawpha or Narayan's Malgudi. However, Newmarch believes that it is frequently difficult to distinguish between the "real" Botswana—that is the one that Bessie Head lived in—and the created Botswana. Perhaps one of the reasons for this difficulty is that she has created—or treats—Serowe (not, significantly,

---

1. It is not unusual for justices to serve limited terms on Botswana.
2. Sesana and Others *v.* the Attorney-General [2006 (2) BLR 633 (HC)], High Court, Lobatse, Botswana, 2006.

the Kalahari or even Gaborone) as a microcosm of a larger Botswana; she extrapolates from what she knows about Serowe, always looking at a larger picture. Newmarch believes that it is important, when considering this problem, to see Serowe (and Botswana) as what he calls an "affirmative marker" (443) in Head's work. What is the Botswana that Head and Dow are creating? They are creating a Botswana where justice is possible, and what Newmarch calls an affirmative marker could be seen as an environment in which this justice can happen, even if it does not yet exist.

Head had a very strong need for continuity—of history, of self, of consciousness (Newmarch 443–44)—and this continuity was both available to her and created by her in Serowe, in her autobiographical and fictional writings (and hence the difficulty of distinguishing between them). The "sense of wovenness" ("For Serowe: A Village in Africa" 30) that so many critics identify in her Botswana work is absent, according to Newmarch, from her pre-Botswana work, which he believes demonstrates more a jumble of subjects, not surprisingly, since she was very unhappy in South Africa. Serowe sustained her as a writer, and even though she remained ambivalent about her allegiance to the nation (Newmarch 445), it nevertheless became the subject, in some way, of her writing: "Botswana is quite as much the *vehicle* as it is the *tenor* of her writing" (444, emphasis in original). He clarifies that "there are indications that she saw Botswana as determining not just the setting or the substance for her writing, but also its voice, or address" (447). In this way, Newmarch states, Botswana is important to Bessie Head not just as a place, but as an idea.

Head's need to create an idea of Botswana as a place where social justice is possible, her perception of what is possible in Botswana, is significant to almost every aspect of her writing. If she does create her own Serowe and even Botswana—and I believe that Newmarch is correct, and not just about *A Bewitched*

*Crossroad*—then she does the same thing for her own life.[3] She knew almost nothing about her own family, and her writing can be understood as an attempt to make a place for herself both physically and socially, for example by creating a mother-hero (like Margaret Cadmore Senior in *Maru*) from whom she can draw strength and inspiration for the difficulties of her own "real" life: "[My mother's] name was Bessie Emery and I consider it the only honor South Africans ever did me—naming me after this unknown, lovely, and unpredictable woman" (preface to "Witchcraft" 72). First, what Bessie Head imagines her life to have been, and second, what she imagines Botswana to be and what potential she sees it to possess, are two aspects of the same issue. In her writing, she needed to express her hope and belief in something better than what she saw around her, problems she captured in her writing but problems she did not let overwhelm her characters. The same can be said of Unity Dow.

This chapter begins with Newmarch's thesis of Botswana as an idea, based on the way that Bessie Head and, to a lesser extent, Unity Dow construct the place—its habits, its beliefs, and its people—for their own critical projects. If Botswana is an idea, then how do these writers present the idea of the place that is different to the way other writers present the place? With the exception of Dow's second novel, *The Screaming of the Innocent*, Botswana in fact becomes a repository of their hopes for social justice, but in order for that justice to happen, injustice first needs to be exposed and interrogated.

In the 1960s, Head was a relative newcomer to Botswana, and she wrote *When Rain Clouds Gather* from that perspective. Here is her first sentence: "The little Barolong village swept

---

3. See Ann Langwadt, "Continuity and Roots: Bessie Head and the Issue of Narrative Identity in Fiction and Autobiography."

right up to the border fence" (7). This sentence gives a sense of life: first of all, it is a village, inhabited; it also "sweeps," giving us a sense of movement and activity. It also sweeps because the border between Botswana and South Africa cuts right through the traditional lands of the BaRolong people, so that immediate family members, although closer to each other than to the next village, are separated by an international boundary. Unity Dow refers to *motshela-kgabo*, or "monkey crossings": "Monkey crossings, that is, jumping over the fence like a monkey, were common because that was the only way Bakgatla could go back to their land, across a political border they had never really accepted....The crossings were called monkey crossings also because the Bakgatla's totem is the monkey" (*Juggling Truths* 87). Head's sweeping village, therefore, makes a number of political and social references: there is life, yes, but it is life divided and manipulated.

After waiting patiently in the hut of an old man, Makhaya[4] grabs his chance to go over, and on the other side of the fence, he finds himself in the bush:

> The air was full of the sound of bells, thousands and thousands of bells, tinkling and tinkling with a purposeful, monotonous rhythm. Yet there was not a living thing in sight to explain where the sound was coming from. He was quite sure that around him and in front of him were trees and more trees, thorn trees that each time he approached too near ripped at his clothes. But how to explain the bells, unearthly sounding bells in an *apparently unlived-in wasteland*? (11, emphasis added)

This is not the bush of adventure, nor is it the beautiful place of McCall Smith. The bush here threatens Makhaya: the bells

---

4. Makhaya is from a Zulu word, *amakhaya*; it refers to those people who are at home.

are unexplained and give an eerie tone to the passage; the thorn trees grab at Makhaya's clothes.[5] The sound in fact comes from cowbells, as Makhaya later learns.

Still later, Makhaya walks along the path, "just his own self" (16), watching the sunrise. He considers the emptiness, which he describes as very beautiful, and wonders if he "confuse[s] it with his own loneliness" (17). Head here possibly describes her own feelings upon arrival in Botswana: as an outsider, she might have found it difficult to make friends, and the memories of the alienation she experienced in South Africa would have been fresh in her mind. Emptiness and loneliness are not necessarily the same thing, and this Botswana is, at first glance, a place of both. But Makhaya's confusion contrasts with his later sensitivity when, for example, he "glanced up briefly, was struck in the eye by a vivid sunset skirt of bright orange and yellow flowers and was momentarily captivated by a pair of large bold black eyes" (78). The land becomes inextricably tied up with the people who live, work, and die on it, and even in this empty wilderness, Makhaya is very soon picked up by a truck driver who asks him if he has been at the cattle post. Thus is he drawn into the people's lives.

This relationship between the desert and the people who live there is consistently maintained throughout the novel, exemplified in Maria's remark to Makhaya: "'You may see no rivers on the ground but we keep the rivers inside us. That is why all good things and all good people are called rain. Sometimes we see the rain clouds gather even though not a cloud appears in the sky. It is all in our heart'" (168). This relationship

---

5. When Isaac jumps off the train in *When We Become Men*, he is injured by the thorns he lands on (10); Makhaya, like Isaac, also comments on tribalism ("He knew some pretty horrifying stories about tribal societies and their witch doctors…" [*When Rain Clouds Gather* 11]). A number of other comparisons between the novels is possible.

is maintained throughout Head's trilogy, in fact. In *Maru*, for example, she writes that "There had never been a time in [Maru's] life when he had not thought a thought and felt it immediately bound to the deep centre of the earth, then bound back to his heart again—with a reply" (7). For Margaret Cadmore the younger, the women who walk past her window to fetch water also "fell in with the sunrise and the sunset, and her quiet dreams at night" (94). This sentiment finds its fullest and final expression at the end of *A Question of Power*, when Elizabeth famously "placed one soft hand over her land. It was a gesture of belonging" (206). What Head's characters strive for, like Head herself, is belonging, continuity, a place to be alive. This need is captured poignantly near the end of *When Rain Clouds Gather*, when Makhaya finds Paulina's son's bones at the cattle post and considers the environment that contributed to his destruction (the social system of boys herding cattle, the drought, the ants that have picked the bones clean), and in that same moment gives in completely to his love for Paulina, taking over responsibility for disposing of the remains and retrieving the small wood carvings that the boy has made. The boy's death is made to carry the weight of love and the people's need for each other. In other words, the drought on the land is tied to the death of Paulina's son, but also the love of the land—its beauties as well as its dangers—is tied to the love that human beings share with one another.

Victoria Margree, in an analysis of how Bessie Head conceptualizes social and political health in her novels, believes that the phrase "pathological normality" best describes Head's understanding of Botswana life, that what we see in these novels is "not an absence of normality but the overstabilization of normality in defence of a life only precariously maintained" (19): "I read Head as conceiving of healthy existence in terms of creativity and openness to change, of unhealth as consisting in an overstabilization that excludes change, and of thinking that these definitions are true for all human beings in all cultures since they are true for all that is *alive*" (20, emphasis in original). Head presents to us, then, the necessity for change, the belief that stagnation is unhealthy. Life changes when Makhaya loves Paulina, when Maru marries Margaret, and when Elizabeth embraces Motabeng. "Normality" only ever exists in the past, since it is based on standards established in the past, but in an idealized past that has also changed over the course of time. For Head, and for Dow, Botswana is not just a hot, dry place because the love that people have for one another redeems them and their physical environment (the rivers within).[6] Of course, it cannot be said that "all you need is love"; the ending of *Maru*, for example, is too problematic to allow that answer, but it goes a long way toward making life easier more generally.

Unity Dow's first novel *Far and Beyon'* (2000) describes the AIDS epidemic in Botswana and the implications of that epidemic for the future of the country. In *Far and Beyon'*, the love that people have for one another has been overwhelmed by the changes brought about by modernity. Although Mosa, the protagonist, is clearly a modern woman (Mosa is short for *mosadi*, meaning woman), she understands that the path to resolving the problems that her family faces involves bringing her family back together. Mosa's family is no longer a family, and she believes very strongly that in order for them to heal after the deaths of two brothers, they must come together again as a family, with love in their hearts. Dow also uses the problem of the culture clash, more specifically the struggle between traditional and modern ways, to explore both the problems that women face within traditional patriarchal society and the difficulties that the society faces in combating the disease.

---

6. Leloba Molema comments that "with such an outlook there is no room for caricatures like the 'stupid, happy African'" (message to the author).

The society of *Far and Beyon'* is Botswana, not a general African one or even a general southern African one. For Dow, one of the most significant problems in the society, one that has frightening implications for halting the spread of AIDS, is the gender hierarchy as it is integrated into Botswana culture. She uses funerals of AIDS victims in particular to identify these problems. Nobantu Rasebotsa discusses this aspect of the novel in more detail:

> Frequent funerals in Unity Dow's text are used as representations of the impact of HIV/AIDS on the lives of Batswana. The lives of the characters are tightly woven with those of the community, so that personal thought and experience are constantly intruded upon by the psychology of the community.
>
> The importance of the community and the nature of Setswana culture is demonstrated by the rituals performed at Pule's funeral and other funeral rites following the burial. Not only is it the pain and grief that Dow's characters are burdened with but also the cultural need to pursue traditional witchcraft methods to hunt down the killer and thereby protect the families from further destruction. (54)

Rasebotsa here identifies an important point about what is positive in Botswana society. Dow's protagonist Mosa understands that the community itself is a central support in the fight against AIDS, even as it divides people from each other by the belief in witchcraft, but she also makes clear that the gender imbalances of that same community contribute to the spread of the disease. Rasebotsa writes, "Through the representations of sexuality within the Botswana patriarchal culture, Unity Dow suggests that the community is caught in a bind because it celebrates male sexuality. Yet the grip of AIDS challenges the community to recognize the need to reevaluate male sexuality" (54). Dow offers a female protagonist who seeks a way to fuse traditional strengths with a "Western" understanding of the disease as a virus as well as a gendered explanation of why things in Botswana are the way they are: she shows clearly that an uncritical return to the "old ways" still divides people—men from women, friend from friend, and more generally powerful from powerless.

In a very telling and central passage, Mosa confronts her brother about AIDS, witchcraft, and their mother:

> "Stan, it is pretty obvious that Mma believes we have been bewitched, right? Hopping from diviner to diviner over the last three years. Sometimes I have gone with her and sometimes I have not. Sometimes you too have been there....Some have dug up evil medicines supposedly planted by enemies. Others have declared that baptism in their church is the only way out....And some of the treatments were outright harmful as far as I'm concerned. But I live with mother and you don't. You cannot take away her belief without replacing it with something else. If I accepted that they were going to die anyway, how would it help her if I told her not to do any of the things that gave her some comfort?"
>
> ...
>
> "Let's take last weekend for example. I think it is fairly harmless. The razor cutting is no more painful than a needle at the hospital. Anyway we all already believed that we needed to get together and work together as a family. Mma wanted desperately to bring us together, hoping that the ceremony would do just that."
>
> "But, Mosa, it cost P600. Two months salary! And it's not over yet. A cow still has to be slaughtered! A pregnant cow! Jesus! Be serious!" Stan was almost shouting....
>
> "Ask your know-it-all Mr Mitchell how much family counselling costs where he comes from. I bet you he will tell you it is not cheap." (105)

In this incident, Mosa confronts her brother with information that he is unwilling to hear about what has happened to his brothers and what is happening to his family. She does not dispute the costs involved, but she also uses his relationship with Mr. Mitchell, the American teacher with whom he boards, to show him what he has lost by living away from home. Again, Rasebotsa writes that Mosa succeeds in "uprooting Stan's tendencies towards individualism and cultivating the spirit of collective consciousness, a consciousness which the author believes should be sensitive to the cultural practices that encourage the subordination and oppression of women, which in turn fuel the epidemic" (54). Change is necessary and inevitable, but it can best be coped with by the entire community working together, not with hierarchies preserved as they are. The cultural practices that Rasebotsa refers to—generally a lack of respect or even consideration for women, but more specifically male high-school teachers who sexually abuse their female students, men who refuse to use condoms, men who do not take responsibility for their wives or offspring, men who beat their wives because wives are like children and need to have discipline instilled in them, without themselves observing the same discipline—support a social system that promotes irresponsible sexual behavior. Preservation, or what Margree calls overstabilization, leads in these scenarios (of *Far and Beyon'*, *Mhudi*, and Head's novels), to stagnation and literally to death. Dow's suggestion—that solutions for problems such as HIV/AIDS must come from a combination of modern critique of gender roles and old-fashioned spiritual strength found in the community—offers a more constructive consideration about the changes that are taking place in Botswana right now. Her perspective on the relationships between men and women is both critical and sympathetic, and her protagonist Mosa understands that neither simply following old rules nor simply ignoring them will help people cope with the changes that modern life brings with it. In this way, she also reminds us of Torontle's Dineo (of *The Victims*), who values both traditional and modern knowledge.

Everything Mosa does, from getting an HIV test to going after the teachers at her school who are sexually preying on pupils, represents an effort to empower the dispossessed and to alter the patterns of the past.

It is important to remember when considering Mosa's relationship to her traditions and to the modern society that she is presented as a modern character, one who holds largely (if not exclusively) with modern understandings of disease, relationships, and such. Her statement that the purification ceremony is "fairly harmless" suggests that she does not believe that such a ceremony can offer anything more concrete to her mother than a vague psychological comfort. She is willing to participate in such rituals for the comfort and peace of mind they offer her mother, but she does not ultimately believe that they can have any other meaning. Her position in this way undercuts her role as a transition figure between tradition and modernity, since she herself seems to sit squarely on the side of modernity. Modernity wins at the "fairy-tale" end of the novel, too, when a governmental *deus ex machina* takes up Mosa's campaign against teachers who sexually harass their pupils. Nevertheless, what Mosa sees as having gotten lost in the transition to a modern life is the sense of togetherness, the compassion for fellow human beings that ultimately enables us all to survive.

Dow has created a strong female protagonist who resists conventional, conservative pressures without losing sight of what is valuable to her as a Motswana: her family and her community. Dow's main characters, like Plaatje's Mhudi, Umnandi, and Hannetje, are all women who aspire to or in fact do work within their communities for change and social justice; they are both more and less than the fearsome creatures described by Sesinyi and Baruti. They challenge the gender norms that many—both men and women—rely on for their social success, but they also respect those aspects of their tradition that hold communities together. In *The Victims*, Dineo's mother warns that "'no man is different. Any man can make you pregnant and desert you. Forget about them until you are in a position of strength, that is, when you are educated enough to stand on your own if need be'" (123). Respect for tradition does not mean that one has to accept being treated as a throw-away source of pleasure.

*Far and Beyon'* offers a number of interesting aspects for readers. The entire first chapter, in which the funeral rituals for Mosa's brother are described in detail, gives an inside view about why things are done the way they are in contemporary Botswana society. Details about public opinion are noted, such as the way HIV/AIDS is spoken of but never referred to:

> Mara [Mosa's mother] had not expected any other expla-
> nation for the death of her son. Thabo too had died from
> a "long illness". The murmuring which followed was to
> be expected. Such vague words as "long illness" always
> meant something was being hidden. Mara thought she
> heard someone say the word AIDS but she could not be
> sure. In any case she could not imagine anyone being cou-
> rageous enough to utter that dreaded acronym, especially
> at a funeral; "this disease", "the radio disease",[7] "*phamo
> kate*",[8] or "the disease with a short name" were the more
> acceptable synonyms. (12)

This secrecy surrounding the disease, the reluctance to talk about it and to name it (usually the cause of death is identi-fied at a funeral), is present in Alexander McCall Smith, too. Caleb Nondo, in *Lethal Virus*, tries to confront head-on the fear

---

7. AIDS is sometimes called the radio disease because people first heard about it on the radio.

8. *Phamo kate* is a shortened form of *phamola katela*, which means to grab something quickly and unexpectedly (*phamola*) and then drop it into a hole and quickly bury it (*katela*). It is an expression that is localized to the area where the BaKgatla live, around Dow's home village of Mochudi.

of AIDS that is represented by the reticence described in the passage above.

The description of the trees in Mara's environment and how she wonders about them (49) also recall Dineo's explanation of the *mophane* trees to Tom. Mara considers the rumors about her neighbor, who was said to have planted a *mosalaosi* tree, a Persian lilac, which is called the tree that stands alone because it sucks all moisture and nutrition from the soil, making it impossible for anything else to grow in its vicinity. As she considers the cycles of the trees' life, she wonders if they, too, suffer nervous breakdowns (49). This sort of information makes the novel a cultural, as well as literary, experience.

Dow's second novel, *The Screaming of the Innocent*, deals more specifically with modern challenges to traditional ways; here, in fact, tradition is the clear enemy. Like the Precious Ramotswe novels, *The Screaming of the Innocent* laments some of the changes that have taken place in Botswana society, but it also laments the tenacity of some of the old ways, and Amantle Bokaa is nowhere near the careful, circumspect Precious Ramotswe. Amantle is a familiar breed of rebel, a young woman who wants to see justice done and who will not hesitate to bend the law to ensure that people who have been mistreated can get a fair shake. In *The Screaming of the Innocent*, Amantle, a young female *Tirelo Sechaba* (national service)[9] participant, discovers the evidence from a *muti* murder (ritual murder for purposes of

---

9. *Tirelo Sechaba* ("service to the nation") is the name given to the national service that used to be required of all school-leavers before they could enter university. The goal was to send participants to areas of the country that they were not familiar with in order to help them understand the situation of the nation as a whole and to instill in them a sense of responsibility for Botswana's well-being. Due to certain issues, including corruption of the sort Amantle describes, *Tirelo Sechaba* was abolished by the government in 2000.

witchcraft) that took place a number of years earlier in the town where she is completing her service.[10]

The novel opens with a description of a man who is observing the victim for the *muti* murder he has ordered to be performed so that he can have his witchdoctor create the strengthening medicine that he needs to succeed in his business endeavors:

> He bore her no malice. He simply wanted her, needed her. Surely, in needing and wanting, there's some affection, even if not quite love....
>
> No, he bore her no malice: not by way of hating her, and not by way of wishing to cause her or her family members pain. He simply wanted her, needed her—the pain was inevitable. (1)

Already in these very first lines, Dow asks us to consider the nature of love in this situation. The man in the car is trying to use love in some way to justify what he is about to do, but it is not the love that shows compassion for others and that prevents the sort of crime that is pending from ever taking place. At first, the little girl is just a little girl, skipping rope and ironically singing a song to chase witches away. The man's life is offered up in more detail, and we see him in a web of relationships: he is described as a good father—his own young daughter is in the car with him and eating an ice cream while he observes his victim—and a good husband. He is a public figure because of his business success. The question implicit in this description is the nature and extent of goodness and evil in any society; even Amantle asks herself as she is driving through the bush, "'How can so much beauty coexist with so much evil?'" (175). The extent of the cover-up of the original murder, the public

---

10. Lauri Kubuitsile's second Kate Gomolemo novel (*Murder for Profit*) also concerns *muti* murder, still a very real occurrence in southern Africa.

standing of those involved, the role that fear plays in keeping people quiet who do not have much power or other leverage, but who know what is going on—these are the issues that are raised by the character sketch of Mr. Disanka as he watches his victim skip rope.

Much of *The Screaming of the Innocent* is devoted to the "detection" of the original details of the crime. In classic *Columbo* style, the novel opens with the impending crime and sketches of the perpetrators, and takes the reader step by step, with carefully planted hints and foreshadowings, through Amantle's new investigation into the death of Neo Kakang. The detective here is a complete, but very intelligent, amateur; the crime has been covered up by high officials in the government; nevertheless these very facts make it imperative that the original circumstances of the crime be brought to light (there is an interesting symbolic torch that appears in connection with Disanka's own daughter, and metaphors about light abound throughout the novel). First, people like Amantle must become aware of the depth of public, social, governmental complicity; and second, the structure of a society in which something like this could be allowed to happen must be interrogated. As Amantle herself goes deeper into her investigation, she remembers an incident from her childhood, in which her own grandmother was suddenly accused of being a witch. One of the neighbors raced forward to defend the grandmother:

> "You despicable snake! Come out from the crowd!! This woman is no witch, and you all know it! Perhaps she wandered into Mma- Soso's yard because she's losing her sight; perhaps she went there to ask for something—but did you give her a chance to explain? No! And you two,"—she directed her anger at the two women, sisters from another ward, who'd dragged Amantle's grandmother to the *kgotla*—"you came all the way from Rapotsane Ward, a ward populated by nasty, spiteful people, to come and cause

all this trouble! And perhaps you should be asked what you're doing in our ward so early in the morning: perhaps *you're* the witches, you good-for-nothing *mafetwa*[11]." (174)

Amantle remembers the speed with which her confused grandmother was accused, and how easily innocent mistakes could be interpreted as hostile or even malevolent.

The role of fear is explored and described in great detail, including in the title *The Screaming of the Innocent*. One of the killers is enticed into participating by quiet attempts to bribe him: the persistence of the attempts eventually frightens him enough that he collapses under the pressure, and he lives with Neo's screams continually echoing in his head. Some of the police officers who handled the original investigation are easily persuaded to drop the matter because they fear the power of men who do not hesitate to commit such crimes. One of the officers, Monaana, tries "to hold back tears," but he cannot hide his fear: "'How can I just say I didn't see these things? I asked for a transfer as well, but was told I'd be working with you to make sure things stayed under control. Sir, I'm afraid too. I don't want to be involved in ritual-murder cases'" (71). Even worse, "[e]ver since the box of clothes had disappeared, he'd been having frightful nightmares" (73). The rediscovered evidence itself (the box of blood-stained clothes) instills fear in those who see it. Amantle occasionally expresses a different sort of fear, too, that efforts to reopen the investigation will fail, and finally there is guilt that results from people who know that what happened was wrong but are too afraid to say anything. Such fear prevents people from acting to change the status quo, and so the situation continues.

Part of the fear undoubtedly stems from a Tswana belief— still quite common—that every death is caused: either one is

---

11. A *lefetwa* (plural *mafetwa*) is an old maid, one who has been "passed by."

bewitched, or one is being punished, or there is some other explanation. Social fear of death and its inevitability, and the possibility that some person has power over life and death, is illustrated very clearly in the story of Amantle's grandmother (172–74). In this incident, the "fairly harmless" belief in traditional power that Mosa (in *Far and Beyon'*) is willing to indulge her mother in takes on a sinister quality when people are ready to convict—condemn—a person despite the possibility of other truly harmless explanations. A strengthening ceremony is harmless because, literally, no one is harmed. *Muti* murder, or *dipheko* (murder for powerful charms), is extremely dangerous, and insidious because of the secrecy that surrounds it and the fear that it instills.

The vehicle for *The Screaming of the Innocent* is the detective genre, but there is a strong moral here—as in McCall Smith—and Dow's narrator does not hesitate to state her opinions and perspective about every aspect of the case and how it is handled. Tradition really is the enemy here. Dow de-romanticizes traditional village justice, and the novel gives other examples of the failure of tradition: one man expects that his case will be heard once he has received four lashes, but the headman departs after the lashing; it seems that "justice was to be meted out in irregular and unpredictable instalments" (13). Amantle observes that allocation of *Tirelo Sechaba* participants is more like a cattle auction, and then finds herself assigned to a host family that expects her "to help care for the whole family" (41) in addition to her work at the local clinic. On her first day, the patients waiting outside the clinic inform Amantle that the nurses never open the clinic on time, and do not do their jobs if they do not feel like it—and abuse the patients into the bargain (45–47). Even Naledi, a newly qualified lawyer who investigates the files of the Kakang case in the Prosecution Division of the attorney general's office, comments on the fact that "if employees showed enthusiasm for a job, it was usually a prerequisite for not getting to do it. Naledi was convinced that this culture whereby the powerful thwarted the desires of the less powerful wasn't limited to her profession..." (124).

*The Screaming of the Innocent* is probably based on Dow's experience hearing similar cases at the High Court, and in fact there are numerous references to Botswana's most famous *muti/dipheko* murder: in 1994 (the year that Neo Kakang disappears), Segametsi Mogomotsi, a fourteen-year-old girl from Mochudi, was found murdered with some of her body parts excised. Rioting followed, with people believing that the police had, at the very least, messed up the investigation or, at the very worst, had perpetrated a cover-up. Eventually Scotland Yard was asked to investigate, but their findings were inconclusive. This is, however, only the most famous case. Anecdotal evidence abounds of people whose children have been "killed by a crocodile" and whose bodies were never recovered, of people whose bodies are found without certain organs or other body parts, and Dow mentions these as well. Boitumelo, the attorney who helps Amantle reopen the investigation, remembers the case of a girl who was convinced that her father had sold her to *muti* killers.[12] Her research in that case led her to believe that "the circumstances surrounding Neo's disappearance, the fruitless search for her, the community anger, the official position taken were all too familiar" (105). She wondered if the killers in the former case had found another victim, and she "had been unable to read about a child killed in a crocodile attack, a train accident or a fire without wondering whether the authorities had been covering up a more sinister cause of death" (106).

Unlike *Far and Beyon'*, or even the later novels *Juggling Truths* and *The Heavens May Fall*, *The Screaming of the Innocent* does not

---

12. Even I know of cases where mothers frantically searched for children who had been sold off for such purposes by their fathers.

have a hopeful ending. We are left to wonder about the need for power and success and the social value placed on them such that horrific crimes like this can continue, when crimes against women and children are not always considered "real" crimes (133). The violence that is embedded in Botswana society, indeed in any society, is not only evident in *muti* murder, and so attacking only one aspect of that violence will not solve the larger problem. Neo's mother remembers a time when Rra-Naso, the man who has been her friend since the disappearance of Neo, was much stronger, when he led an attempt to beat the madness out of his nephew. The boy was beaten bloody, but the "cure" did not take, and he remained tied to his tree, where he had been kept before the attempt (178–79). At the end of *A Question of Power*, Elizabeth addresses the nature of this sort of violence when she says that "[s]ince man was not holy to man, he could be tortured for his complexion, he could be misused, degraded and killed" (205); and clearly not only for complexion can one be killed, but for anyone else's weakness or fear of something different. Fear, and the weakness that it engenders, lead to the injustice that Dow sees daily and decries in *The Screaming of the Innocent* and elsewhere.

Dow's third novel, *Juggling Truths*, is about growing up in a rural society in Botswana around the time of independence— symbolically important, of course, as the narrator and protagonist Monei tests her own independence as she progresses through primary school. This is a girl who wants to make decisions about how things in her own life ought to be run: she wants to be in charge, but she has no female role models, so her secret ambition is to be the Queen, the only person who does such things *and* is a woman (44). The title of the novel refers to the problems of a young girl who learns things at school that do not seem to fit with what she knows to be true from home; her friend Frieda refers to them as school truths and real truths, and explains this concept to Monei as follows: "'Look Monei, what's

written in books is school truth. What is spoken and is obvious
is the real truth. That is why, although my real name is Lesego,
at school I'm called Frieda. That is the name in the book'" (83).
Much of the novel is centered around such real or home truths
and how Monei learns to integrate what she learns at school
and what she knows at home:

> When my grandmother woke me up early one morning
> and told me about the monthly bleedings, I realised that
> there were some school truths that were also home truths.
> After the talk, she told me to take a broom and to brush
> over my chest as I leaned over the large clay pot at the
> back of the rondavel where we slept. This was to sweep
> away the small buds of breasts I had started to sprout.
> This would delay their growth and postpone the onset of
> the bleedings for months, perhaps even years. There was
> no need to hurry into adulthood, she told me. (86)

An important point in this education is that her family supports
her investigations, always finding an explanation that is both
correct and *fair*.

*Juggling Truths* is structured more anecdotally, rather than
following a conventional plot line, and Monei is more of a
bridge or transitional figure (between "home" and "school"
truths) than is, for example, Mosa of *Far and Beyon'*. The plot
is Monei's life during her primary school years, but there is
no beginning, middle, and end in conventional terms. Rather,
Dow takes events from the narrator's life and devotes a chapter
to them, in which Monei explains to readers what happened,
why these things were said to happen, what she believed about
them, and what had to be done to resolve them. *Juggling Truths*
is a delightful mine of information, and every story in it describes an aspect of life. Monei begins by explaining her place
in the web of familial relationships, how the passage of time in
her family is marked by the seasons as she understands them

(not the English seasons, which belong to the category of school truths), how people understand Jesus and their ancestors, and how they choose ways of making both sets of belief viable for their own lives. The book is full of questions about how life happens. One notable passage occurs after Monei fails to pass her tests to be baptized in the Dutch Reformed Church:

> Where is Hell exactly anyway? Heaven, it seemed to me both Christians and the entire village agreed, was obviously up in the sky. You did not have to go to church to know that it was where one ended up after death—except that the missionaries had introduced Jesus as some kind of gatekeeper. But is hell next to heaven? Is there a wall dividing the two? Will we be able to hear the screams of the people roasting in hell? If you get tired of eternal life, can you like leave? I mean like die? Maybe commit suicide? Where will you go if you kill yourself in heaven? I tried to keep these thoughts out seeing as they were responsible for my not being baptised with the rest of my *Phuthagwana*[13] classmates. I briefly considered enrolling in the Catholic Church's catechism class but the persisting rumours of the Kokoto Father's shameful praying habits stopped that thought long before it matured into any serious plan. (161–62)

Monei describes a conflict that is not unfamiliar to people of the region, but her formulation of it seems logical within her own context, as a child coping with both home and school truths, but also contradictions in a postcolonial, independent state: as we read, we become involved in Monei's life, and the reader shares her experience of trying to cope with unsatisfactory answers that do not seem to add up. But as Monei sorts them out we see her as someone who can create Botswana's new future.

---

13. *Phuthagwana* is a Mochudi term that describes a group of people who are preparing to be baptized.

This future, the fairness that characterizes Monei's family's behavior, is epitomized in the prevalence of sensible female figures. Monei's grandmother is possibly the most important figure in her life, and the grandmother's comments about a particular event, situation, or issue punctuate Monei's narrative. However, Monei's mother Marata is also an important role model for Monei: although a woman, she is frequently asked for advice, and even "uncles consulted her on male topics, while pretending to indulge her in her need for gossip" (30). In Monei's world, women and their contributions are accommodated within the patriarchy— a contradiction that is full of possibility, rather than repressive, as in *Far and Beyon'*, or even threatening, as in *Carjack*. So Monei grows up in a household where the opinions of women matter, resulting in a very ironic commentary at the end of the novel, when Monei has passed her exams, thus convincing her brother that he should go to school, too: "At first my father was reluctant" but "[t]imes were changing and my father was persuaded" (172). A common trope in such *Bildungsromane* by women is that they must persuade their fathers that girls should go to school, too.[14] Dow puts a humorous twist on the need for educating both girls and boys, and thus the possibilities of the future open up to everyone.[15]

Dow's most recent novel, *The Heavens May Fall*, is a more straightforward critique of the legal system of Botswana—not only of what it does to women but also of how it fails to allow for *everyone* to be heard. The narrator/protagonist, Naledi Chaba, is an attorney for a nonprofit organization that defends

---

14. This trope is possibly best represented in the region by the opening line of Tsitsi Dangarembga's novel *Nervous Conditions*, "I was not sorry when my brother died" (1), because she is then able to go to school.

15. In Botswana, unusually for the region, more girls than boys were sent to school, since herding cattle—a boy's job—was seen as more important than getting an education.

victims of domestic abuse, frequently underage women who have been raped; thus, it is not surprising that the novel focuses on the status and difficulties of women in Botswana society. There are very few men who do not come under heavy fire from Naledi and her friend, Dr. Mmidi More (an administrator at Deborah Retief Memorial Hospital in Mochudi), but part of the story that is told by Naledi is of the importance of learning to listen to everyone, including men, who may behave in a particular way because of things they do not know. Refusing to listen is but another way of shutting people out of participation, of keeping them powerless, of perpetuating social injustice.

The main story or problem, only introduced at the midway point of the book, concerns a man whose mother is a San and who has been passing as a MoNgwato his whole life. The clash of cultures represented by that man's life is echoed in other situations of the novel as well: a woman wants legal help in persuading her husband to undergo a traditional cleansing ceremony in order to exorcise the *thokolosi* that his mother has sent to rape her every night; another woman cannot understand why in her divorce she is not allowed to keep the house in which she lived with her husband because she does not want the husband's new wife to sleep on the graves of her dead children, who are buried under the marriage bed—even though she does not want the property on which the house sits, since that rightly belongs to her husband's family. The culture clash between the BaNgwato and the San, however, has repercussions beyond individual situations: San are believed to be incapable of the sorts of things that other members of Botswana society aspire to, and so for this man's background to come out would rock Botswana society. Dow is of course familiar with the problems of San in contemporary Botswana society, since she was one of the presiding judges for the case concerning the relocation of San from the Central Kalahari Game Reserve (in which she ruled in favor of the San's claims). Her awareness of the situation is summed up in the following passage, in which the man's mother tells the story of his upbringing and describes what it is like to be a "bushy": "'Sometimes, as I go about my domestic duties, fetching water, collecting firewood, going to the shops, I see faces with the tell-tale slanted eyes and light colouring, but they look away quickly, afraid to acknowledge me. I understand. It is not easy. Hiding is better'" (180). As Naledi listens to this story, and considers her role in nearly creating more suffering for those involved, she recognizes the role her own stereotypes have played in the way the events have unfolded, and concludes "that the main lesson I had learned from the desert trip was '*audi alteram partem*', 'hear the other side'" (191).

Unfortunately, Naledi's newly enlightened outlook is somewhat overshadowed by the tone of the novel as a whole. Like *Juggling Truths*, *The Heavens May Fall* is episodic, but each episode serves to enforce the idea that Naledi and her friend Mmidi are the only two people in Botswana who work for social justice; every episode introduces the reader to more unsavory and sleazy characters, so that we begin to wonder what the point of it all is. Of course, the point is that one does have to consider the other perspective, but the conclusion is not forceful enough to stand up to the onslaught throughout the novel of horrible things perpetrated mainly by men.

An important point of comparison between Bessie Head and Unity Dow emerges here. Bessie Head, famous for her numerous statements that "I'm not a feminist," really is not, at least not in the Western understanding of the term. Head recognizes the capacity to abuse power that exists in every human being, and she writes about the struggle within human beings—most famously summed up in her statement that "there was no guarantee against the possibility that I could be evil too" ("Some Notes on Novel Writing" 63). Dow's outlook is unabashedly female, probably reflecting her own dedication to the causes of women's empowerment. *The Heavens May Fall* strikes a very obviously feminist note in the tireless and beleaguered efforts of Naledi Chaba to right all the wrongs that are perpetrated by men against women. However, this most recent novel seems to catch itself (although perhaps not quite soon enough to ameliorate the harsh tone of self-righteousness that runs through the rest of the novel) in the story of the prominent man who is "really" a San. The novel starts by lamenting that women's complaints are ignored, but it ends with a plea to listen to all who suffer injustice. Dow reintroduces those qualities from her first three novels: to really institute justice, people have to keep their perspectives very, very broad. Naledi Chaba learns just in time that she "could be evil too." What makes Botswana women exceptional (to use the term) is the belief, articulated by Dow, Head, Mositi Torontle, and Sol Plaatje, that women carry the best hope for a better society, that their strong sense of community makes it less likely that they will leave anyone behind in the march toward a better future.

David Newmarch draws a distinction between the real and imagined Botswana in Bessie Head, but all of the novels discussed in this chapter contain a promise about hope for the sort of Botswana that is possible, one that looks to the old morality of Mma Ramotswe and even of Andrew Sesinyi, but one that is based on the idea that following tradition does not preclude changing what is unfair. Power relations—be they defined in terms of race, sex, adult versus child, government bureaucracy versus citizen, or any combination of these—are defined, by Head and by Dow, as corruptible, and therefore immoral. The idea of Botswana that Newmarch identifies for Bessie Head is present in both Head and Unity Dow: it is a Botswana in which morality means not just knowing what is fair and just for all, but in applying that knowledge in all aspects of one's life.

# CONCLUSION

> The history of African literature in French could be summed up as a progressive (if still incomplete) seizure of *the means of projection*, a transfer of the right to represent Africa in French, from French writers to Africans. This leaves Western readers on the outside, forced to come to terms with their difference. (Miller 296)

Although a book about novels of Botswana written by a white American woman may not seem an obviously appropriate step in transferring rights of representation to Africans, I hope that the preceding overview has raised questions and, more importantly, interest in how Africans, in this specific case Batswana, are engaged in representing themselves, and how their own representations might offer more useful insights into this foreign—in the sense of "not my own"—culture. Western readers need to look at African writing—all of it, not just the works that are designated as "worthy"—

161

to understand more completely the context of what they are reading about.

What do the Batswana themselves write about? What is important to them? They are most centrally concerned about morality and its role in defining "Tswana" identity: this identity relies very heavily on, among other things, cultural memories of the *kgotla* and the peaceful, democratic nature of precolonial and colonial chiefs, a memory that lives on in how Botswana praises its own peaceful democracy today. How accurate these memories are is of course open to debate: many stories, poems, and oral accounts of earlier years reveal an extremely violent side of Botswana society, and the egalitarian nature attributed to *kgotla* participation glosses over the realities of *who* was allowed to participate and to what extent *kgotla* meetings were orchestrated to validate certain opinions and decisions. Botswana's own sense of its exceptionality, demonstrated in the affirmation of these old or "traditional" values, finds voice in much popular literature, as well as in much of what is published in current newspapers. The persistence of these ideas demonstrates that Batswana understand their own lives in ways that refer not only to their colonial and postcolonial past, but also and most significantly to ideas about themselves that they want to collectively "remember"; these ideas do not always connect with the "modern" life that characterizes Gaborone and that many see as a legacy of Western domination. The debates are dynamic and contemporary: at the time this book was finished, modernity, tradition, and neo-traditionalism characterized an ongoing legal conflict between the chief of the BaKgatla, Kgafela, and the constitutional government.

For the West, Botswana is the land of the Okavango Delta and the Kalahari Desert, sparsely if at all populated, but also a "bastion of democracy" in an autocratic, kleptocratic, violent, poor continent. Most Western writers of Botswana only barely see the people around them, shadows who enable or hinder the West's own quest for self-identity, an identity that seems to exist on the other side of a journey across this sandy or watery desert. The best among Western writers look up from the ground and find themselves surrounded by people who have their own sense of themselves, one that is not merely peripheral to the project of the Western quest for identity. In spite of their flaws, the Precious Ramotswe novels consider the "nature" of the people who live in the delta and the desert. What do they think? How do they understand their relationship to their society and, most importantly, to their nation Botswana? How do they perceive outsiders, like myself? What are the ethical tenets on which they base their behavior?

For Batswana, the ethical tenets arise from their history; for many Western writers, those tenets seem to arise from the land itself: violent, empty, beautiful, conquerable. Fighting the landscape to clarify one's own place in the world—ironically in a foreign country—or to bolster the forces of good, usually democracy, in these cases or examples ignores the fact that for these visitors, morality is defined elsewhere: "what is good is what I need; it supports my world and my life elsewhere." These ways of thinking leave no room for friendly curiosity about other inhabitants of the earth.

Foregrounding the Batswana, either in writing by Batswana or in writing by for example McCall Smith or Caitlin Davies, leads to an entirely different view of morality from the one that develops in Western novels, one that was originally introduced to readers in the work of first Plaatje, then Sesinyi, Baruti, and Torontle, and one that begins to be interrogated in Head and Dow. The evolution of literature both within and about Botswana offers possibilities for an inward examination of the cultural myths and memories that are such an important part of Botswana's own self-identity, especially as a peace-loving and fair nation. Head and Dow raise questions that start to address the not-so-fair foundations upon which Botswana's reputation rests, even if the reputation is largely accurate. History is not only the stuff we want to remember.

Botswana's image of itself depends more on its people and on maintaining a myth of status, peacefulness, and "rightness" that is lacking from most outside writers. Botswana Defence Force (BDF) Day is held every year at the end of April and offers both an orgasmic display of military skill and machinery but also a good amount of general, rather circus-like, entertainment, including clowns. After the 2008 celebration of BDF Day, *Mmegi* (in an article by Gale Ngakane) ran an article describing the events that were staged in Francistown. The day ended with a mock battle that epitomized Botswana's self-image:

> [T]here were two sides, a place of peace and tranquility where people went about their duties while on the other side of the divide burst of gunfire and commotion was a daily occurrence.
>
> Matters came to a head when people from the turbulent side of the border, aptly named *Matsubutsubu* (Upheavals) crossed the border to the tranquil side, aptly called *Thokgamo* [uprightness, integrity] to kidnap women at a shebeen. (3)[1]

The stage names of the two countries leave no doubt as to the better nation: *Thokgamo* is not merely free of upheaval, it is also the "right" and correct—moral—place.

Botswana's image of itself can also be understood to some extent according to a gender perspective: men want to go back to a more static kind of old tradition, although they set their work almost exclusively in the new, modern, capital city of Ga-

---

1. The contemporary reference to the land of upheavals is most probably Zimbabwe, but before 1990, the reference would have suggested South Africa and the cross-border raids by the apartheid government's destabilization forces. Also, *Matsubutsubu* was translated in the article; *Thokgamo* was not.

borone, where no one comes from. Their attitude is not surprising, given that Botswana still has strong patriarchal habits that reinforce the higher status of men. Nevertheless, women are moving up the hierarchy, and women writers frequently write about the problems that characterize the lives of the subordinate, and they tend to set their writings in villages where people really come from. A writer like Sesinyi, by looking at the modern manifestation of the Botswana national ethic in the Botswana national capital, affirms the structure of old relationships (such as feudal, class, etc.), but the transposition of these relationships into the modern city of Gaborone stresses traditions to the point that they themselves contribute to the moral decay that Sesinyi laments in his novels. Christopher Miller, writing of *Les soleils des indépendences* by Ahmadou Kourouma, says that "[t]his belief in an eternal ethnic and family structure…forms the backbone of [the character's] attitude. It is an attitude that directly contradicts the stated goal of most postcolonial African regimes, building a national identity by transcending, if not superseding ethnic affiliation…" (238). Ironically women look to a more "national" identity in Miller's sense, both in terms of place and in terms of status, and thus expose the power relationships that threaten the same national identity. The "belief in an eternal ethnic…structure" also forms the backbone of Sesinyi's characters, but it is an unacknowledged backbone, invisible, and because of its narrow definition all the more threatening to the national project. When the backbone, the structure, is exposed, in the writings of Head and Dow, for example, the idea of a "national identity" takes on a broader perspective. Their approach is equally risky because the threat that their writing poses to the status quo is clearer and more overt, and while their critique threatens to overwhelm their desire to preserve what is good, their outlook is also perhaps more robust and more honest.

In recent years, more and more people have begun to write: the University of Botswana has added a Media Studies

Department to the Faculty of Humanities, training writers as well as other media specialists in the art of representing their world. Self-publishing has become popular, and many newspapers have again begun to publish poetry submitted by their readers. More and more literature prizes have appeared on the scene, including one sponsored by Alexander McCall Smith, another by the Bessie Head Heritage Trust, and others sponsored by cellular network providers. The Writers' Association of Botswana has once again become active, joining the UB Writers' Workshop in mounting readings by members, and poetry nights (Exodus, Live Poets) are a popular feature at many clubs around Gaborone. Such events seem to herald increased literary activity in Botswana, as Botswana continues to define itself as a nation and to expand regional relationships with other southern African countries and global relationships in an increasingly connected world.

After this book was completed, a number of new novels came out, and the number of novels published continues to increase. Unfortunately they could not be included here; they are listed in the appendix.

Writing this book has been a multiyear project. Over the course of those years, I have been living in the very place I have been reading about, interacting with the very people I have been trying to get to know through the literature, comparing my own experiences with what I read in this fiction. Any discussion of these books does not come near describing the pleasure I have derived from reading even the most predictable novels about Botswana and the people I have come to know, admire, and love. I wish others the same pleasure.

# APPENDIX: NEW PUBLICATIONS SINCE 2007

Davies, Caitlin. *Black Mulberries*. London: Simon and Schuster, 2007. Print.

Gurganious, Thokozile. *The Government's Child*. Lexington, KY: Xlibris, 2009. Print.

Harvey, Lionel. *Do As Botswana Does*. Gaborone: Pula Press, 2007. Print.

Kubuitsile, Lauri. *Murder for Profit*. Gaborone: Pentagon Publishers, 2008. Print.

Makgala, Christian John. *The Dixie Medicine Man*. New York and Bloomington: iUniverse, 2010. Print.

Mbo, Nsununguli. *Wrong Turn*. Bedfordshire, England: Authors OnLine, 2009. Print.

—. *A Crisis of the Heart*. New York and Bloomington: iUniverse, 2010. Print.

McCall Smith, Alexander. *Miracle at Speedy Motors*. London: Little, Brown, 2008. Print.

—. *Tea Time for the Traditionally Built*. London: Little, Brown, 2009. Print.

—. *The Double Comfort Safari Club*. London: Little, Brown, 2010. Print.

—. *The Saturday Big Tent Wedding*. London: Little, Brown, 2011. Print.

—. *The Limpopo Academy of Private Detection*. London: Little, Brown, 2012. Print.

Mojokeri, Phidson. *Curse of a Dream*. Gaborone: Pentagon Publishers, 2009. Print.

Ndlangamandla, Masa P. *If I Could Speak*. Gaborone: Books Botswana, 2008. Print.

Ntumy, Cheryl. *Crossing*. Gaborone: Pentagon Publishers, 2010. Print.

Ontebetse, Khonani. *Born with a Husband*. Gaborone: Pentagon Publishers, 2008. Print.

Senau, Tshetsana. *Travelling to the Sun: The Diary of Ruth*. Gaborone: Pentagon Publishers, 2011. Print.

Seretse, Gasebalwe. *The Pursuit of Xhai*. Gaborone: Books Botswana, 2008. Print.

Sesinyi, Andrew. *Shadows of Birth*. Gaborone: Media Palms, 2010. Print.

Stanley, Michael. *A Carrion Death*. New York: HarperCollins, 2008. Print.

—. *A Deadly Trade*. London: Headline, 2009. Print.

—. *Death of the Mantis*. London: Headline, 2011. Print.

Sőderstrőm, Gaafele. *The Lost Son of Mochudi*. Gaborone: Gaafele Sőderstrőm, 2011. Print.

Tlalanyane, Phemelo. *Journey to Bogofi*. Gaborone: Books Botswana, 2008. Print.

Tsheko, Refilwe. *Twists and Turns*. Gaborone: Pentagon Publishers, 2007. Print.

# WORKS CITED

*48th Miss Universe Pageant.* Trinidad and Tobago. 26 May 1999. Videotape.

Agbaw, S. Ekema and Karson L. Kiesinger. "The Reincarnation of Kurtz in Norman Rush's *Mating.*" *Conradiana* 32.1 (2000): 47–58. Print.

Bagnall, Sheila. *Sheila Bagnall's Letters from Botswana, 1966–1974.* Ed. Sandy Grant. Oodi, Botswana: Leithlo Publications, 2001. Print.

Baruti, Galesiti. *Mr. Heartbreaker.* Gaborone, Botswana: Botsalo, 1993. Print.

Bennett, Bruce. Rev. of *The No. 1 Ladies' Detective Agency* and *Tears of the Giraffe* by Alexander McCall Smith. *Marang* 12–13 (1996–97): 43–44. Print.

Björnson, Richard. *The African Quest for Freedom and Identity: Cameroonian Writing and the National Experience.* Bloomington and Indianapolis: Indiana UP, 1991. Print.

Bowen, Mark. Rev. of *The Great Thirst.* New York Times. 17 Nov. 1985. BR30. Print.

Busia, Abena. "Manipulating Africa: The Buccaneer as 'Liberator' in Contemporary Fiction." *The Black Presence in African Literature.* Ed. David Dabydeen. Manchester and Dover, NH: Manchester UP, 1985. 168–85 Print.

Butler, K. R. *A Desert of Salt.* New York: M. S. Mill & William Morrow, 1964. Print.

—. *The Evil Damp.* London: Geoffrey Bles, 1966. Print.

Coetzee, J. M. "Jerusalem Prize Acceptance Speech (1987)." *Doubling the Point: Essays and Interviews.* Ed. Davit Attwell. Cambridge, MA: Harvard UP, 1992. 96–99. Print.

Cole, D. T. *An Introduction to Tswana Grammar*. 1955. Cape Town and Johannesburg, Longman Penguin Southern Africa, 1992. Print.

Dangarembga, Tsitsi. *Nervous Conditions*. Seattle: Seal Press, 1989. Print.

Davies, Caitlin. *Jamestown Blues*. London: Penguin, 1996. Print.

Dinesen, Isak (Karen Blixen). *Out of Africa*. 1937. Middlesex: Penguin, 1954. Print.

Dow, Unity. *Far and Beyon'*. Gaborone, Botswana; Longman, 2000. Print.

—. *The Screaming of the Innocent*. 2001. Cape Town: Double Storey Books, 2003. Print.

—. *Juggling Truths*. 2003. Cape Town: Double Storey Books, 2004. Print.

—. *The Heavens May Fall*. Cape Town: Double Storey Books, 2006. Print.

Duggan, William. *The Great Thirst*. 1985. London: Arrow Books, 1986. Print.

—. *Lovers of the African Night*. New York: Delacorte, 1987. Print.

Easthope, Antony. "Writing and English National Identity." *Contemporary Writing and National Identity*. Ed. Tracey Hill and William Hughes. Bath: Sulis Press, 1995. 146–57. Print.

Eilersen, Gillian Stead. *Bessie Head: Thunder Behind Her Ears. Her Life and Writing*. 1995. Johannesburg: Wits UP, 2007. Print.

Fleischer, Anthony. *Okavango Gods*. Cape Town: David Philip, 1998. Print.

Good, Kenneth. "Interpreting the Exceptionality of Botswana." *The Journal of Modern African Studies* 30.1 (1992): 69–95. Print.

Grant Thornton. *International Business Report 2007: Global Overview*. Web. 12 May 2008.

Gray, Stephen. *Southern African Literature: An Introduction*. Cape Town: David Philip and London: Rex Collings, 1979. Print.

Head, Bessie. *A Bewitched Crossroad: An African Saga.* Craighall, SA: AD Donker. 1984. Print.

—. "The Collector of Treasures." *The Collector of Treasures and Other Botswana Village Tales.* London: Heinemann, 1977. 87–103. Print.

—. "For Serowe: A Village in Africa." *A Woman Alone.* 29–31. Print.

—. *Maru.* 1971. London: Heinemann, 1972. Print.

—. Preface. "Witchcraft." By Head. *Ms.* Nov. 1975: 72–73. Print.

—. *A Question of Power.* London: Heinemann, 1974. Print.

—. *Serowe: Village of the Rain Wind.* Oxford: Heinemann, 1981. Print.

—. "Some Notes on Novel Writing." *A Woman Alone.* 61–64. Print.

—. *When Rain Clouds Gather.* 1968. London: Heinemann, 1987. Print.

—. *A Woman Alone: Autobiographical Writings.* Ed. Craig MacKenzie. Oxford: Heinemann, 1990. Print.

Kakutani, Michiko. "A Midlife Crisis Gets a Full Treatment." Rev. of *Mortals. New York Times Book Review.* 27 May 2003. E7. Web. 7 Aug. 2006.

Klass, Sheila Solomon. "Light a Match and Start a Revolution." Rev. of *Lovers of the African Night. New York Times Book Review.* 20 Dec. 1987. 11. Print.

Kubuitsile, Lauri. *The Fatal Payout.* Gaborone, Botswana: Macmillan, 2005. Print.

—. Message to the author. 17 October 2006. Email.

Kwere, Keamogetswe and Lesie Kwere. "We Will Be Leasing for Ourselves." *Women Writing Africa, Vol. 1: The Southern Region.* Ed. M. J. Daymond, et al. New York: The Feminist Press, 2003. 484–88. Print.

Langwadt, Ann. "Continuity and Roots: Bessie Head and the Issue of Narrative Identity in Fiction and Autobiography." *The Life and Work of Bessie Head: A Celebration of the Seventieth Anniversary of her Birth.* Ed. Mary S. Lederer, Seatholo M. Tumedi,

Leloba S. Molema, and M. J. Daymond. Gaborone, Botswana: Pentagon, 2008. 105–18. Print.

Larson, Thomas J. *Dibebe of the Okavango.* Lincoln, NE: Writers Club Press, 2001. Print.

—. *Hambukushu Rainmakers of the Okavango.* Lincoln, NE: Writers Club Press, 2001. Print.

Leonard, John. "Grand Allusions in Botswana." Rev. of *Mortals. New York Times Book Review.* 8 June 2003. n.p. Web. 7 Aug. 2006.

Lilford, Grant. Message to the author. March 2008. Manuscript.

—. "*Motswana ke mang?* Tswana Culture and Values in Plaatje, Head, and McCall Smith." *The Life and Work of Bessie Head: A Celebration of the Seventieth Anniversary of her Birth.* Ed. Mary S. Lederer, Seatholo M. Tumedi, Leloba S. Molema, and M. J. Daymond. Gaborone, Botswana: Pentagon, 2008. 85–104. Print.

Luard, Nicholas. *Silverback.* London: Hodder & Stoughton (Coronet), 1996. Print.

*Macmillan Social Studies Atlas for Botswana.* 1988. Gaborone: Macmillan, 1995. Print.

McCall Smith, Alexander. *The No. 1 Ladies' Detective Agency.* 1998. London: Abacus, 2003. Print.

—. *Tears of the Giraffe.* 2000. London: Abacus, 2003. Print.

—. *Morality for Beautiful Girls.* 2001. London: Abacus, 2003. Print.

—. *The Kalahari Typing School for Men.* 2002. London: Abacus, 2004. Print.

—. *The Full Cupboard of Life.* 2003. London: Abacus, 2004. Print.

—. *In the Company of Cheerful Ladies.* 2004. London: Abacus, 2005. Print.

—. *Blue Shoes and Happiness.* Edinburgh: Polygon, 2006. Print.

—. *The Good Husband of Zebra Drive.* Edinburgh: Polygon, 2007. Print.

McVean, James. *Bloodspoor.* New York: Dial Press/James Wade, 1977. Print.

Margree, Victoria. "Wild Flowers: Bessie Head on Life, Health and Botany." *Paragraphs: A Journal of Modern Critical Theory* 27.3 (2004): 16–31. Print.

Maughan-Brown, David. "Raising Goose-Pimples: Wilbur Smith and the Politics of *Rage*." *Rendering Things Visible: Essays on South African Literary Culture*. Ed. Martin Trump. Johannesburg: Ravan Press, 1990. 134–60. Print.

Mekgwe, Pinkie. "'All that is fine in the human condition': Crafting Words, Creating Ma-Ramotswe. Pinkie Mekgwe and Alexander McCall Smith in Conversation." *Research in African Literatures* 37.2 (2006): 176–86. Print.

Merriweather, Alfred M. *Desert Harvest*. London: Lutterworth, 1977. Print.

Miller, Christopher L. *Theories of Africans: Francophone Literature and Anthropology in Africa*. London: U of Chicago P, 1990. Print.

Mitchison, Naomi. *When We Become Men*. 1965. Glasgow: Kennedy and Boyd, 2009. Print.

Mizejewski, Linda. *Hardboiled and High Heeled: The Woman Detective in Popular Culture*. New York & London: Routledge, 2004. Print.

Mogae, Festus G. "State of the Nation Address by His Excellency Mr. Festus G. Mogae, President of the Republic of Botswana, to the First Meeting of the Third Session of the Ninth Parliament 'Maturity and Consolidation', Monday 13 November 2006." National Assembly, Gaborone, Botswana. 13 Nov. 2006. Address.

Molema, Leloba. Message to the author. n.d. Manuscript.

Monsarrat, Nicholas. *The Tribe That Lost Its Head*. 1956. London: Pan Books, 1959. Print.

—. *Richer Than All His Tribe*. 1968. London: Pan Books, 1970. Print.

Mwamba, Trevor H. *Dancing Sermons*. Edinburgh: Maclean Dubois, 2006. Print.

Ndebele, Njabulo. *Rediscovery of the Ordinary: Essays on South African Literature and Culture*. 1991. Durban: U of KwaZulu Natal P, 2006. Print.

Newmarch, David. "Bewitched Crossroads: The Problematic of Bessie Head's Contribution to a Literature of Botswana." *Swansea Review* (1994): 429–49. Print.

Ngakane, Gale. "BDF Clowns Thrill F/town Youngsters." *Mmegi* 29 April 2008: 3. Print.

Nondo, Caleb. *Lethal Virus.* Gaborone: Macmillan Botswana, 1997. Print.

Parsons, Neil. "Botswana: An End to Exceptionality?" *The Round Table* 325 (1993): 73–82. Print.

Plaatje, Sol. *Mhudi.* 1930. Johannesburg: Quagga Press, 1975. Print.

Rasebotsa, Nobantu. "AIDS Fiction in Africa." *The Discourse of HIV/AIDS in Africa.* Proceedings of the conference Language, Literature and the Discourse of HIV/AIDS in Africa. Ed. Emevwo Biakolo, Joyce Mathangwane, and Dan Odallo. Gaborone, Botswana: University of Botswana, 2003. 52–57. Print.

van Rensburg, Patrick. *Report from Swaneng Hill.* Uppsala: Dag Hammarskjold Foundation, 1974. Print.

—. *The Serowe Brigades: Alternative Education in Botswana.* Basingstoke: Macmillan for the Bernard van Leer Foundation, 1978. Print.

Robinson, David. "Looking for Mma Ramotswe." *The Scotsman* 21 Aug. 2004. n.p. Web. 3 May 2006.

Rovin, Jeff. *Tom Clancy's Op-Center: Mission of Honor.* Series creators Tom Clancy and Steve Pieczenik. New York: Berkley, 2002. Print.

Rubadiri, David. "The Theme of National Identity in East African Writing." *National Identity.* Ed. K. L. Goodwin. Melbourne: Heinemann Educational, 1970. 51–57. Print.

Rush, Norman. *Mating.* New York: Vintage, 1991. Print.

—. *Mortals.* London: Jonathan Cape, 2003. Print.

—. "Near Pala." *Whites.* 17–31. Print.

—. "Thieving." *Whites.* 32–57. Print.

—. *Whites*. 1986. London: Paladin, 1987. Print.

Ryan, William F. "The Genesis of the Techno-Thriller." *Virginia Quarterly Review* 69.1 (1993): 24–40. Print.

Schapera, Isaac. *The Ethnic Composition of Tswana Tribes*. London: London School of Economics, 1952. Print.

Sesinyi, Andrew. *Love on the Rocks*. London: Macmillan (Pacesetters), 1981. Print.

—. *Rassie*. Oxford: Macmillan (Pacesetters), 1989. Print.

—. *Carjack*. Gaborone, Botswana: Longman, 1999. Print.

Sherlock, Christopher. *Night of the Predator*. London: William Heinemann, 1991. Print.

Silet, Charles. "The Possibilities of Happiness: An Interview with Alexander McCall Smith, Author of *The Full Cupboard of Life & The No. 1 Ladies' Detective Agency*." *Mystery Scene* 80 (2003): 28–31. Print.

Slaughter, Carolyn. *Dreams of the Kalahari*. New York: Charles Scribner's Sons, 1981. Print.

Smith, Wilbur. *The Sunbird*. 1972. London: Pan Books, 1997. Print.

Sullivan, Joanna. "Redefining the Novel in Africa." *Research in African Literatures* 37.4 (2006): 177–88. Print.

Tlou, Thomas and Alec Campbell. *History of Botswana*. Gaborone: Macmillan Botswana, 1997. Print.

Tlou, Thomas, Neil Parsons, and Willie Henderson. *Seretse Khama, 1921–80*. Gaborone: Botswana Society, 1995. Print.

Torontle, Mositi. *The Victims*. Gaborone, Botswana: Botsalano, 1993. Print.

Trinh T. Minh-ha. "Writing Postcoloniality and Feminism." *The Post-Colonial Studies Reader*. Eds. Bill Ashcroft, Gareth Griffiths, and Helen Tiffin. London and New York: Routledge, 1995. 264–68. Print.

Verne, Jules. *Meridiana: The Adventures of Three Englishmen and Three Russians in South Africa*. 1872. Trans. ? London: Sampson Low, Marston & Co., 1874. Print.

White, Steve. *Battle in Botswana*. New York: Warner, 1982. Print.

Willan, Brian. *Sol Plaatje: South African Nationalist 1876–1932*. Berkeley: University of California Press, 1984. Print.

Williams, Susan. *Colour Bar*. London: Allen Lane/Penguin, 2006. Print.

Wylie, Dan. "Elephants and Compassion: Ecological Criticism and Southern African Hunting Literature." *English in Africa* 28.2 (2001): 79–100. Print.

# INDEX

AIDS, see HIV/AIDS

Bagnall, Sheila, 80
Bantu languages, 7
Baruti, Galesiti, 14–15, 28, 131, 163
    *Mr. Heartbreaker*, 28, 42–43
Basarwa, 8
Bechuanaland Protectorate, see Botswana
Bjŏrnson, Richard, 15, 25
*bogadi*, 49n10
Bophuthatswana, 1
*botho* (humanity), 129, 131
Botswana Defence Force Day (Botswana self-image), 164
Botswana
    borders, 13, 17, 139
    colonial government, 22–23, 31
    diamonds, 2
    exceptionality of, 22–24, 50
    history, 9–13, 22–23, 31, 45
    hunters, 10, 91–92, 110
    images of, emptiness, 2–3
    images of, in McCall Smith, 118–19
    images of, modernity in, 24–25n3
    images of, "original Africa," 3
    inequality, 2, 23, 34–35
    minority languages, 11, 12, 16
    missionaries, 10
    name of, 9
    national anthem, 46
    nonracialism, 11, 62n6
    tourism in, 65, 82–83, 105–6, 108

wildlife, attitudes to, 68n9
writing, recent expansion of, 165–66
Bowen, Mark, 73
"Bushmen," see San
Busia, Abena, 92
Butler, K. R., 92
    *A Desert of Salt*, 66, 98–103, 105
    *The Evil Damp*, 103–5

Cameroonian literature, 15, 25
Campbell, Alec, 9n7
Central Kalahari Game Reserve (CKGR), 3, 79n20, 136, 158
Clancy, Tom, 112
Coetzee, J. M., on white South African attitude to land, 113
Cole, D. T., 8n6
Conrad, Joseph, *Heart of Darkness*, 81, 83
courts, traditional, 152

Dangarembga, Tsitsi, *Nervous Conditions*, 157n4
Davies, Caitlin, 163
    *Jamestown Blues*, 64–68
    *Place of Reeds*, 64
democracy
    and traditional government (*kgotla*), 28, 162
    modern, 83, 93, 111, 113, 162
desert landscape
    conquest of nature, 52
    in *Bloodspoor*, 110
    in *A Desert of Salt*, 98–100, 102–3
    in *Dreams of the Kalahari*, 59–61
    in *Jamestown Blues*, 65–66
    in *Mating*, 84
    in "Near Pala," 76–77, 79
    in *Night of the Predator*, 105
    in Norman Rush, 75
    in *The Tribe That Lost Its Head*, 96
    in *When Rain Clouds Gather*, 139–40

Western attitudes, 163
development, 3
didactic writing, 25–26
*difaqane*, 27
Dinesen, Isak, 127, 128n6, 129
Dow, Unity, 15, 17, 163
    career, 136
    *Far and Beyon'*, 142–48, 157
    *The Heavens May Fall*, 157–60
    *Juggling Truths*, 139, 154–57
    *The Screaming of the Innocent*, 138, 148–53
drama, 17
Duggan, William, *The Great Thirst* and *Lovers of the African Night*, 73–74

Easthope, Antony, 14
Eilersen, Gillian Stead, 18
ethnic identity, 5

Fleischer, Anthony, *Okavango Gods*, 68–73

Gaborone, 13n9, 15, 164–65
Gikandi, Simon, 25
Good, Kenneth, 22
Grafton, Sue, 116
Gray, Stephen, 92

Haggard, H. Rider, *She*, 107
Hambukushu, 9
Harry, Prince, 2
Hausa literature, 25
Head, Bessie, 15, 17–18, 163
    and feminism, 159
    and Serowe, 136–37
    *A Bewitched Crossroads*, 17, 26, 29–31, 136, 138
    birth, 138
    *The Cardinals*, 17, 48n9
    *Maru*, 4n4, 17, 72n14, 138, 141, 142

*A Question of Power*, 17, 18, 72, 141, 154
*Serowe: Village of the Rain Wind*, 18
*When Rain Clouds Gather*, 17–18, 113, 138–42, 140n5, 141
*When Rain Clouds Gather*, abridged edition, 18
*When Rain Clouds Gather*, Setswana translation, 18
Herero, 9
HIV/AIDS, 25, 31
 in *Far and Beyon'*, 143–48
 in *The No. 1 Ladies' Detective* series, 123–26
hunters, see Botswana

Kakutani, Michiko, 88n25
Kalahari, see desert landscape, see also Lost City of
Kalanga, 9
Kaplan, Alice, 75n16
Keïta, Fodéba, 5
*kgotla*, 23, 30, 162
Khama III, 22, 49
Khama III Memorial Museum, 18
Khama, Sir Seretse, 1, 9, 23
 marriage to Ruth Williams, 11, 93, 94
Khama, Tshekedi, 10
KhoeSan, see also San
 language groups, 8
Kiesinger, Karson L., 81
Klass, Sheila Solomon, 73
Kourouma, Ahmadou, *Les soleils des indépendences*, 165
Kubuitsile, Lauri, 116, 117–18, 131, 134n11
 *The Fatal Payout*, 131–33
 *Murder for Profit*, 149n10
Kwelagobe, Mpule, 24n2
Kwere, Keamogetswe and Lesie, 3n3

Langwadt, Ann, 138n3
Larson, Thomas J., *Dibebe of the Okavango*, 68n10
Leonard, John, 76, 79
Lessing, Doris, 58–59, 61n4

Lilford, Grant, 17n13, 134n12
literature, importance of context, 5–6, 7
literature prizes, 166
Lost City of the Kalahari, 111
Luard, Nicholas, *Silverback*, 109

Maasai, 4
Mafikeng (Mafeking), 13, 17
Margree, Victoria, 141–42, 145
Maughan-Brown, David, 98n3
McCall Smith, Alexander, 14, 51, 116–17, 147, 160, 163
    *Blue Shoes and Happiness*, 119, 120, 122, 123, 126
    cover images, 134n11
    *The Full Cupboard of Life*, 121
    *In the Company of Cheerful Ladies*, 117, 119, 121–22, 124
    *The Kalahari Typing School for Men*, 121, 126
    *Morality for Beautiful Girls*, 4n4, 119, 120
    *The No. 1 Ladies' Detective Agency*, 118, 120, 127–29
    *The No. 1 Ladies' Detective Agency* films, 2, 134n11
    *Tears of the Giraffe*, 118–19, 126
McVean, James (Nicholas Luard), *Bloodspoor*, 109–10
Mekgwe, Pinkie, 126
Merriweather, Alfred M., *Desert Harvest*, 89–90
Miller, Christopher, *Theories of Africans*, 4–6, 161, 165
Minghella, Anthony, 2, 134n11
Miss Universe, 2, 24n2
Mitchison, Naomi, *When We Become Men*, 52–58, 140n5
Mizejewski, Linda, 115–16
Mochudi, 15
Moffat, Dr. and Mrs., 130n8
Mogae, President Festus, 122n3
Mogomotsi, Segametsi, murder of (1994), 153
Molema, Leloba, 142n6
Monsarrat, Nicholas, 92–93, 94
    *The Cruel Sea*, 94
    *The Tribe That Lost Its Head* and *Richer Than All His Tribe*, 94–98, 99

*morafe*, 28n5
*muti* murder
   in *Murder for Profit*, 149n10
   in *The Screaming of the Innocent*, 149–54
   Mogomotsi, Segametsi, 153
Mwamba, Bishop Trevor, 124

national novels, 24–25
nationalism, 12–14, 165
Ndebele, Njabulo, 26n4
Newmarch, David, 136–38, 160
Ngakane, Gale, 164
*No Sweet without Sweat*, 34
Nondo, Caleb, *Lethal Virus*, 25, 147

Obiechina, Emmanuel, 25
Okavango, see water landscape

Parsons, Neil, 22–23
"passion killing," 131n10
Pieczenik, Steve, 112
Plaatje, Sol, 17, 163
   and Setswana language, 17
   *Mhudi*, 17, 26–30, 41, 146
poetry, 17
postcolonial studies, 5

Rasebotsa, Nobantu, 143–45
refugees
   in *Dreams of the Kalahari*, 61–62
   in *When Rain Clouds Gather*, 139–40
   in *When We Become Men*, 53–54
relativism, 5–6
religion
   in *Juggling Truths*, 156
   in *Mission of Honor*, 112–13
   in *The Victims*, 55
van Rensburg, Patrick, 80n22

Rhodes, Cecil, 10
Robinson, David, 129, 130
Rovin, Jeff, *Mission of Honor*, 88, 111–13
Rubadiri, David, 13–14
Rush, Norman, 52
    *Mating*, 53, 75–76, 80–88, 128
    *Mortals*, 88–89
    "Near Pala," 75–80, 82
    *Whites*, 75, 101n4
Ryan, William F., 112n11

San, 3, 4, 8–9, 98, 106, 105–6, 108, 111, 158–59, 160
Schapera, Isaac, 28n5
school uniforms, well-ironed, 42, 45
Serowe, 15, 18
Sesinyi, Andrew, 14–15, 28, 29, 131, 160, 163, 165
    *Carjack*, 24, 37–42, 49, 115, 157
    *Love on the Rocks*, 23, 32–34, 28, 41, 133
    *Rassie*, 34–37, 41
Setswana language
    classes and prefixes, 7–8
    literature, 15–16, 21
    in South Africa, 16n11, 22
    national language, 11
    representation of in English, 58n2
    "Tswinglish," 66
Sherlock, Christopher, *Night of the Predator*, 93, 105–9, 128
Slaughter, Carolyn
    *Before the Knife*, 58
    *Dreams of the Kalahari*, 58–64, 76, 77n18, 128
Smith, Wilbur, *Sunbird*, 111
South Africa, as "Rainbow Nation," 11
Sullivan, Joanna, 25

themes, see also Botswana, desert landscape, water landscape, women
    colonial enterprise, 96–97

inequality, 34–37
morality, 14, 22, 43, 49, 119–23, 160, 165
self-discovery, 52, 92
tradition/modernity, 32–33, 54–58, 144–46
*Tirelo Sechaba*, 148n9, 152
Tlou, Thomas, 9n7
*tokoloshe (thokolosi)*, 2n2, 158
Torontle, Mositi, 29, 163
    *The Victims*, 44–49, 145, 146–47
Trinh Minh-ha, 81–82

University of Botswana, 9, 18, 32n6, 165–66

van der Post, Laurens, 106n8
Verne, Jules, 112n11
    *Meridiana*, 91

water landscape
    in *Bloodspoor*, 110
    in *The Evil Damp*, 104–5
    in *Okavango Gods*, 69–70
White, Steve, *Battle in Botswana*, 88, 111
Willan, Brian, biography of Sol Plaatje, 29
Williams, Susan, *Colour Bar*, 94
witchcraft, 2n2, see also *muti* murder
    in *Far and Beyon'*, 143, 144
    in *The Screaming of the Innocent*, 150–51
women, 164–65
    in Botswana business, 2
    in *Carjack*, 39–41
    in *Far and Beyon'*, 146–47
    in *The Heavens May Fall*, 157–58, 159–60
    in *Juggling Truths*, 157
    in Lauri Kubuitsile's detective novels, 117–18
    in *Mating*, 84–85, 87
    in *Mhudi*, 29, 40–42
    in *The No. 1 Ladies' Detective* series, 116–17

    sexual abuse in schools, 146
    strong, 117–18, 146–47
Wylie, Dan, 92